Music of
the Heart

Music of the Heart

Roberta Guaspari

with Larkin Warren

NEW YORK

Copyright © 1999 Roberta Guaspari

All rights reserved. No part of this book may be used or reproduced in any manner whatsoever without the written permission of the Publisher. Printed in the United States of America. For information address: Hyperion, 77 West 66th Street, New York, New York 10023-6298.

Designed by Ruth Lee

Library of Congress Cataloging-in-Publication Data

ISBN: 0-7868-8487-8

FIRST EDITION

1   3   5   7   9   10   8   6   4   2

I give this book, with great love

—to the memory of my father, whose presence I feel at every one of my concerts

—to Mom, for teaching me to never give up on something I believe in

—to my son, Nick, whose strong heart, able leadership, and musicality will always make a difference

—to my son, Alexi, whose great sensitivity and ability to see the good in everyone brings joy and healing to the world around him

—and to my daughter, Sophia Estefania, who will keep me young and fighting forever, always in awe of her beauty and strength of character

Starry Night

*I*am standing on the stage of Carnegie Hall. I am standing on the stage of Carnegie Hall. On the morning of
October 25, 1993, these words kept running through
my head. If I had said them aloud, it would have been
with astonishment and a certain amount of awe, for I
was indeed on the stage of the historic recital hall in
New York City, holding tight to my violin and bow as I
looked out at the enormous red-carpeted palace, its
plush seats stretching out and up, into the great sweep
of boxes, tiers, and the wide balcony high above.

Right now, all those seats were empty. By 7:30 that
evening, they would be filled—with members of my
family, with friends, with friends of friends, and hun-

dreds of other people I didn't know. The seating capacity was almost three thousand; the concert scheduled to take place that night had been sold out for two weeks.

As the morning wore on, technicians and stagehands began to gather backstage, looking at the video monitors and leaning over control boards, pushing various buttons and switches. From one side of the hall to the other, lights were blinking on, then off, and every few minutes someone's voice—a staccato *check! check! check!*—bounced up to the ceiling and back down again.

On the stage around me was a Hall of Fame of string musicians, including maestro Isaac Stern; Itzhak Perlman; Arnold Steinhardt and Michael Tree of the Guarneri Quartet; Midori; Ani and Ida Kavafian; Diane Monroe; country fiddler Mark O'Connor; and jazz virtuosos John Blake Jr., Karen Briggs, Billy Taylor, and Dave Grusin. Less well known, but no less important, was a group of younger violinists, ranging in age from eight to eighteen, with names like Melia and Andres, Aaliyah and Kendra, Jairus and Omar, Fabian and Shantha.

They and thirty other kids on the stage were students or graduates of the East Harlem Violin Program, a public-school music instruction program I started in 1980. In the years since, it had grown to encompass three elementary schools, reaching more than 150 kids a year. Recently, however, the city's fiscal crisis had threatened my teaching job and nearly caused the collapse of the violin program. Only the dedication of the students' parents and our friends had kept the program and my hopes alive; in fact, the concert that night was a benefit for Opus 118 Music Center, the violin program's nonprofit support organization.

With great pride and a stomach full of butterflies, I watched "my kids" rosin their bows and prepare to rehearse. I remembered putting their first violins in their hands—hands that were much smaller then, with chubby little fingers—and guiding them, one awkward note at a time, all the way through *Twinkle, Twinkle, Little Star*. Now, in just a few hours, they would share music stands with some of the world's finest musicians and play their hearts out in everything from *The Orange Blossom Special* to Bach's *Double Concerto*.

The very first concert ever held at Carnegie Hall, which celebrated its centennial in 1991, was conducted by Tchaikovsky. Paderewski performed here; Dvorak's *New World Symphony* premiered here, as did George Gershwin's *Concerto in F* and Duke Ellington's *Black, Brown and Beige*. Gustav Mahler and Philip Glass; the Beatles and the Rolling Stones; Frank Sinatra and Miles Davis—all of them and many others had stood right where I was standing. Tonight, to my great amazement, we would become a part of that history.

As the bustle of preparations continued around us, the intensity and focus that each musician poured into the rehearsal actually seemed to raise the temperature in the great hall. Barely a year before, we thought we were finished: The budget was cut, the money was gone, the kids and their violins were about to be silenced.

Give it up, some people said—this is happening in public schools all over the country these days, and that's just the way it is.

But we didn't give up. We fought back. And now it seemed we were on our feet, surviving, even (almost) thriving, in the company of the generous musicians who had joined in our fight. In some ways, the concert could almost be seen as a victory celebration.

But I knew it was far too early for that. As proud as I was—proud to be in this company, proud of what we had done and were about to do—I was no longer as naïve about happy endings as I once was. Too many problems still weren't solved; too many questions remained unanswered. As I looked out into that empty auditorium, imagining how glorious the music would sound later that night, I was truly excited to be on that stage.

And I knew that we all still had a long, long way to go.

Music of
the Heart

First Notes

*T*he first time I ever held a violin, I was in the fourth grade—which is pretty late, the neuroscientists tell us, if I had entertained any dreams of growing up to be a Perlman or a Heifitz. Fortunately, my nine-year-old self only wanted to know how to make the lovely instrument work, and how to make beautiful music come out of it. As any parent of a beginning violinist will tell you, the "beautiful music" part would take a little time.

My first violin, and the lessons that went with it, came as they did for most American children in the fifties—in public elementary school. I was one of those kids who was always the first to raise my hand with an answer or an idea, so when I was asked by a visitor to my school (who examined my hands and pronounced them big) if I wanted to learn how to play the violin, I enthusiastically volunteered.

I was raised in Rome, a town in upstate New York, in the Mohawk River Valley. Known as the birthplace of the Erie Canal, Rome was surrounded by Revolutionary War monuments. Fort Stanwix, the site of a famous British siege in 1777, is right in the center of the city. The author of the Pledge of Allegiance, Francis Bellamy, is buried in a local cemetery.

As rich as Rome was in historic tradition, my family's life and history seemed much more compelling to me. I was the oldest of four kids (brothers Al and Doug, little sister Lois) brought up in the middle of an extended, noisy, working-class Italian Catholic family, with almost everyone we were related to within reach of a voice or a hand. The Vitalis, my mother's side of the family, lived right next door—Dad's side, the Gasparis, were only a few blocks away.

Grandpa Vitali left Italy for New York when he was about sixteen. More than ten years later, he was walking through a Rome park when he saw my future grandmother, a girl not yet twenty, sitting in a swing. That was all he needed. "I just liked the way she looked," he always said.

Grandpa owned the land our house was built upon; my mother's sister, Aunt Eleanor, and her husband built a house next door—my cousin, Marie, was like a sister to me. For a while, my mother's other sister, Aunt Mary, her husband, Gus Trotsky, and their son Joe, lived upstairs in my grandparents' house. Starting with my grandfather, there were so many Giuseppes—the Joes— among all the uncles and the cousins that the only way we could tell the difference between them in conversation was by using their middle names in combination with their first names, all at once. There was JoeSteven, JoePeter, and JoeTrotsky (no middle name)—too many Joes to count.

A born gardener and cook, Grandpa taught his young bride everything he knew; in turn, she taught everyone else, and woe be unto any daughter or daughter-in-law who used shortcuts in the kitchen. In Grandpa's garden there were cherry trees, fresh tomatoes and green beans (we called them pole beans), and a large, tangled grapevine with a picnic table underneath. There was a wine cellar, braids of garlic hanging everywhere, and fresh basil, oregano, and mint in the greenhouse.

My father, Guido (known as Guy), built the house we lived in. A furnace mechanic for the Revere Copper and Brass Factory, Dad maintained and repaired the furnaces that produced metal alloys for everything from the familiar Revere saucepans to construction and industrial products. The factory was just across the parking lot from our house; from the front door we could see the huge, red neon Paul Revere riding his horse on top of the main building.

My father was a perfectionist at work and at home, a "by the rules" man and an artist as well—an odd and sometimes exasperating combination. There were few things Dad didn't know how to do, and our house was a prime example. With my uncles' help, he had poured the foundation, then went on to build the walls, the roof, and almost everything inside: the brick chimney, the carved mantel over the fireplace, the kitchen cupboards, and the Ping Pong table. One of Dad's most ambitious projects was a bowling alley ball-delivery ramp in the basement, built to scale, with fitted tongue-in-groove oak, a banked return against the opposite wall, and the same varnish the Rome bowling alley used. He and my brother Dougie practiced spot bowling down there for hours. After that, he said, it was all in the delivery.

Dad was musically talented—he sang in a barbershop quartet and a German choir. He also loved to sketch and draw, and invented a cast of cartoon characters and the stories to go with them. After school (his shift at the factory ended at 3:30), my friends would come over and ask him to draw the pictures that illustrated his tales of Little Red Dopeyhead, who was always getting into very funny trouble.

Dad had been a lifeguard in the navy, so we were all taught to swim "by the book"—the Australian crawl, the breast stroke, with careful attention to the proper name and form for each. He loved to fish, and often took us trout fishing up on the Mohawk River, complete with hip boots and casting rods. He tied flies that were so delicate they looked like jewelry; it was almost hypnotic to watch him tie the miniscule knots.

Nothing was ever done partway—when Dad got into

health food, he read everything Adelle Davis ever wrote, bought a juicer, and made a daily goopy preparation that we called his "concoction": carrot juice, lecithin, brewer's yeast, and blackstrap molasses. It looked disgusting (which is why he made few converts), but he swore by it.

My parents were careful with money and completely unpretentious about how they lived their lives, but they went all out at Christmastime. My mother baked for days in advance—Italian butter balls, and chocolate and cherry cookies, many of them carefully decorated with white, green, and red frosting. Nothing but the perfect Christmas tree would do, and it seemed to take Dad forever to decide which tree passed the test. After he got it home, he would trim the branches in such a way that the manger he had built seemed to nestle there, its roof covered with precisely placed cotton snow.

On Christmas morning, my brothers and sister and I would walk into an ordinary living room that in one night had been magically transformed into a child's dream. Our presents, organized in four separate groups, were arranged in a display that looked like a holiday window in a fancy Fifth Avenue department store. They were often unwrapped and accompanied by a note from Santa himself, penned in impeccable calligraphy.

Like everyone on the Guaspari side of the family, my dad was an avid consumer of books. Although he never went to college, he knew the works of the great philosophers and poets. He had set aside a special learning area in the basement, with a blackboard upon which he wrote a saying every week, often from Plato or Aristotle. Even in the midst of her most determined house cleaning, Mom knew that she couldn't ever erase that blackboard without checking with Dad first.

If we had trouble with a subject in school, my father would tutor us. If it was a subject he knew, he drew from his own knowledge; if it was something he was unfamiliar with, he promptly went out and found the right book. In fact, it was Dad who taught us about the birds and the bees. I can still remember the drawing on the blackboard: fallopian tubes, ovaries, uterus. He did it with such matter-of-factness that I was only mildly embarrassed.

The downside to his stubborn pursuit of excellence was, of course, that everything took forever—and there was almost no way to escape the process. The Christmas tree took days; the bowling alley took weeks. And my siblings and I knew that whenever we went down to the basement with Dad for a tutoring lesson, it would be hours before we would come back up again. Patiently and precisely, he would start each time at the beginning, and we'd think, *Oh, no, here he goes.*

When he came home from the war, Dad married his little sister Norma's best friend, Assunta Vitali. While she may not have had the head for books and arcane philosophy that Dad did, my mother shared his eye for quality and the belief that no effort was too great for the family. She was proud of our house, and polished its furniture and buffed its wooden floors until the surfaces were blinding. Her primary artistry, of course, was her cooking. She always used fresh ingredients from Grandpa's garden, with everything, from soup to pastry, made from scratch. She rarely cooked for fewer than ten people. In fact, fifteen or twenty people at the dinner table was not unusual; the smells of sautéed garlic and onion drifting out through the windows in the afternoon drew the aunts and uncles and cousins right in. Ten dozen ravioli at a time? No problem—she spread the cheesecloth across her bed, and there the fresh pasta would dry.

With a natural talent for mathematics, Mom was also the family banker. At any given time she knew how much money was coming in, what had to be paid out, and how to save anything left over. She always had the numbers calculated down to the last nickel, and she kept the figures in her head. She was a tireless bargain hunter, forever returning things to stores after she had taken a second look at them at home, determined that no one would ever take advantage of her or her family by selling her second-rate merchandise.

When I was thirteen, Mom got her first paying job, as dining-room attendant at a local residence for disabled people. She scrubbed and polished there, too, and then came home to cook and bake for a full house. I know now I could have helped her out more, but I was much more likely to be practicing the violin—in the kitchen, right in front of the refrigerator—while Mom made endless detours around me, moving the music stand each time she had to open the refrigerator door.

"But the sound is better here," I protested when she suggested I go elsewhere in the house. "It's more resonant!"

"Let the girl practice," insisted my dad. "Let her play."

My parents were not educated people, at least not in terms of universities or degrees, nor did they travel much beyond Rome, New York, but they taught us indelible lessons. They seemed to take as great a joy in the process of a task, the *doing* of it—the woodworking, the baking, the day-to-day crafting of their life with their children—as they did in the end results. And at the heart of everything was love of family, which in their case had a particular kind of Italian fierceness about it.

I knew at an early age that no matter what road I pursued when I grew up, family would be, must be, central to everything I did—followed closely, of course, by the insistence on excellence and a determination to never do anything halfway. I will always be grateful for the example they set me, but opinion (both in my own house and among my students) is divided as to whether this perfectionism is a blessing or a curse!

My music teacher from the sixth grade through high school was Willard Mathers, who taught both the junior-high and high-school orchestras. In time, he would teach the rest of the Guaspari kids—Al on string bass, Dougie on cello, and Lois on violin and then viola. A devoted Catholic and father of seven, Mr. Mathers was connected to our community in a deeply profound way—even in our general adolescent obliviousness, his students sensed that commitment. He knew all of us, he made it a point to know our parents, and he had a kind of radar for who needed a little toughness and who needed a gentler hand. He often drove me home after orchestra practice, and usually Mom invited him to stay for dinner. When he did, I listened spellbound as he and my father discussed philosophy and spirituality, and the importance of making moral choices in life.

For someone who obviously loved his work and his students, Mr. Mathers could also be quite strict. He had no tolerance for wasted time—talking or goofing around during practice could get you singled out in a very un-comfortable way. "Stop noodling!" he'd demand if some-one was fooling with an instrument while he was trying to get us to focus and pay attention. The message was clear: He took music seriously and expected us to do the same. These days, when I scold my own students with a sharp "Stop plucking!" I hear the echo of Mr. Mathers's voice.

He always arrived at orchestra practice in a coat and tie. In a few minutes, the coat came off; moments later, he loosened his tie. By the end of rehearsal, he was so wringing wet his undershirt was clearly visible under his white dress shirt. This was my first real exposure to the dynamic of the "open circuits" that can connect students and teachers, where the energy flows back and forth at such a level that it's almost palpable. He passionately wanted us to get it right, to feel the joy that comes with achievement, and we knew it. In return, we wanted him to be pleased with us—we wanted to meet his expectations and be rewarded with the look on his face when we did. Like a power plant, Mr. Mathers sent the gift of his great energy out to us, and we fired it right back at him.

In the seventh grade, when I wanted to quit—because orchestra "wasn't cool"—he asked me to give it another six months, promising to arrange some great music. He was as good as his word, coming up with a number of Beatles songs, and a rafters-rattling version of *Hello, Dolly!*, which our school orchestra later performed for audiences at the 1965 World's Fair in New York City. When I thought about quitting a second time, in high school—to be a cheerleader, to have long fingernails—he would have none of it.

"Oh, for heaven's sake, Roberta, be a cheerleader with short nails," he said. "But there will be no quitting." He knew that the way I had come to feel about the violin and music would eventually win out. Of course he was right.

Ask most baby boomers who play instruments today (either recreationally or professionally) how they began, and they, too, will often recall the earliest days of elementary school. Conductor Leonard Slatkin, of the National Symphony Orchestra in Washington, reports that he discovered the possibilities of hands-on music in Los Angeles when a visiting music teacher, armed with an autoharp, came to his classroom twice a week.

In his recent book *Indivisible by Four*, violinist Arnold Steinhardt, celebrating thirty-five years with the Guarneri Quartet, tells of experiencing the same West Coast beneficence as Slatkin did. "At the age of six," he writes, "I knew I wanted to play the violin. For a two-dollar deposit, the California public-school system provided me with an instrument."

A lot has been made of "the golden age" of music instruction in America's schools. Some purists have argued that maybe it wasn't so golden after all—the instructors were often underqualified, the instruments were far from perfect, the level of teaching was uneven, and the results were never quantified in any reliable, statistical way. But the fact remains that there was a time in this country when exposure to music and the opportunity to learn to play it was widely available and relatively cheap for American kids.

The real golden age of music education was immediately after the Civil War, when every town had a band, every school had band uniforms, and music lessons and recitals were part of almost every child's education. Before that time, music education in school was primarily vocal—glee clubs and choral societies were a natural outgrowth of church choirs. By the 1920s and 1930s, however, music was an integral part of the public-school classroom. Inter-school band competitions were as eagerly attended as football games, and state championships in the various musical specialties were as coveted by school districts as athletic trophies were.

Ironically, music education began to wind down just as the boomers were getting their first taste of it, in the mid-1950s, when the Cold War and the arms race created an increased emphasis on science and technology. If anyone needed convincing, Russia's launch of Sputnik I, in October 1957, did the trick. Dr. Edward Teller, the "father" of the hydrogen bomb, warned that the country had just lost a battle "more important and greater than Pearl Harbor." Senator Henry Jackson said the launch was a defeat of "the prestige of the U.S. as the leader in the scientific and technical world." American kids had to arm themselves for a new kind of competition, and not with violins or paintbrushes.

Luckily for many of us, it took another twenty or thirty years and a couple of serious recessions before the deepest cuts in arts programs took effect in our school districts. The days of everyone being handed a musical instrument were coming to an end, but a potential music student could usually find a source for lessons at school. In my own case, I never even had a private lesson until I went to college.

Perhaps it may have been different if I had been some kind of child prodigy or if my parents had been pushing me toward a performing career, but that wasn't the case. A professional musician? That wasn't practical, my father insisted—and besides, he had a much better idea.

My parents were above all traditional, with all the expectations (especially for their daughters) that that implies. Yes, of course, they said, play the violin. Make music, draw, and paint. Be an athlete—do gymnastics, play baseball (I was a switch-hitter) and basketball (I actually won a free-throw contest in Rome during junior high school), dive, swim. Do whatever you can do to enrich your life. Explore all the possibilities—and in the end, remember this: The most important thing a woman can do is find a good husband, be a good wife, and raise good children. If a career is what you want in addition to a family, then of course, you must do it. So why not be a teacher?

Given the great respect for teaching and learning I was raised with, I could think of nothing more honorable to strive for. It was a practical choice, but it had the challenge of creativity written all over it. Teachers influence and mold children. They maintain quality and excellence and standards in their communities. They pass on precious traditions *and* they introduce new ideas. And they have summers, vacations, and evenings to be with their families. Yes, I thought—I will be a teacher, and I will teach the violin.

These days, I often hear people say that for them, high school was a miserable experience. Now that I've taught school for most of my life and raised my own children, I understand what they mean. Adolescence can be a treacherous time, and self-esteem is a fragile thing. But

I wouldn't have understood any of that when I was a teenager. I was pretty, enthusiastic, and talented at many things, and within the confines of my large (and watchful) family, I could do no wrong. In fact, even when I *was* wrong, my family backed me up. My mom's younger brother—my Uncle JoeSteven—said to me one day, "Bert, I know that whatever you put your mind to do, you will succeed."

In high school, I was supposedly going steady with the football captain, but we were off as much as we were on. He and I had a deal: If we stayed "broken up" for more than ten days, I was then free to go out with other people. We would get to day seven, day eight, and his friends would start teasing him in the halls. "Is it time yet? Can she go out with somebody else yet?"

There was someone else who kept track of the breakup days, a boy who teased *me* with "Is it time yet?" His name was Brian.* From the time we were in junior high until we graduated from high school, Brian was a constant, attractive presence in my life. We played in the school orchestra together (he played the trombone) and we were in some classes together. We were in the same classroom—honors English—the afternoon that President Kennedy was shot.

His father had died of a brain tumor when Brian was a baby, and his brother had been killed in a sledding

---

*To protect the privacy of the individual and the family discussed here, this name is a pseudonym and will be used throughout the book.

accident. His mother was a teacher, a very well-read and educated woman who had seen more than her share of sorrow. She was raising Brian and his older sister with a firm hand. They had what I thought of at the time as class, and it had nothing to do with money.

An observer didn't have to look too closely to see the differences between us—I was obviously Italian, Catholic, and blue-collar working class; Brian was a middle-class WASP, handsome and popular, headed on to bigger things long before we graduated. That didn't stop him from flirting with me; it didn't stop me from flirting right back, looking at him every once in a while and thinking, *Hmm, I wonder.* . . . Even Mr. Mathers noticed. He gave me a rough time about dating someone who wasn't a musician. Why, he teased, wasn't I going out with that nice Brian?

Although I did well in math and science, I struggled in the honors English class. Reading serious literature—analyzing, philosophizing, reflecting—involved a different kind of thinking for me than playing the violin did. "What does this poem mean?" would mean spending hours with the thesaurus—or my father. I succeeded in holding a 90 average, but I just about killed myself to do it.

Most of the students in that class were brilliant, ultimately scoring very highly on the SATs; my own scores barely scraped past 500. Many of them were headed for the Ivy League after graduation. My cousin, David Guaspari (who graduated sixth in our class of more than seven hundred) was going abroad to Cambridge University, where he would eventually receive a doctorate in mathematical logic. Brian was going off to Amherst College. He knew that he wanted to pursue a career that helped people in some way. He thought that might be the ministry, which meant theological study after he completed his undergraduate degree.

I was headed for Syracuse University, for a degree in music performance and to study with the famous Louis Krasner. Thanks to Mr. Mathers, my SATs didn't carry as much weight as the musicianship he had helped me achieve: I was not only accepted to Syracuse, I was informed after my audition that I had earned a full scholarship.

My college plans took an abrupt turn when Governor Nelson Rockefeller decided to take a closer look at his state budget, especially the amount allotted to education. Although Syracuse is a private university, the grant source for my scholarship came from state funding. The governor, while trimming his budget, trimmed away my scholarship as well. It was my first hard lesson in bureaucracy, budget cuts, and the need to always have a Plan B.

It was quickly decided that I would attend the State University of New York—SUNY—at the Fredonia campus, which was five hours away from home. Not only was the tuition manageable for my family, the music department there had a very good reputation. As I began to prepare for the next phase of my life, my parents, grandparents, aunts, and uncles were all cheering me on. And maybe, in addition to getting a fine education

(I seemed to hear everyone suggesting), I would find the perfect husband as well.

These days, if parents and grandparents were to openly link college achievement to the hunt for Prince (or Princess) Charming, the student in question would probably pitch a fit. When my own two sons went off to college a few years ago, they were no doubt in search of many things, but I don't believe that "wife" was on either of their lists (or, at any rate, at the top). But when I was eighteen, the ultimate success—according to the belief system of all the people I loved, whose approval I craved—was defined as marriage and family. Teaching music—or whatever career I decided to pursue—was an acceptable, even desirable, adjunct to that goal. But marriage, and the right partner, came first.

And I didn't disagree with any of that. Unlike many of my friends, I wasn't rebelling against anything, although I certainly had strong opinions and wasn't afraid to express them. I had inherited my mother's passion for all things domestic and my father's passion for all things artistic. The combination made me a prime candidate for every Happily Ever After cliché there was, even as the women's movement began to percolate somewhere off in the distance.

Enter the Prince

I had so much to learn at Fredonia—*and where the vi-olin was concerned,* so much to relearn. In my first ten years with the instrument, I had played with all my might, with passion, energy, spirit, almost always *con gusto.* But because I never had a private lesson until I was eighteen, I didn't have the technical training that would have helped me build a stronger foundation.

In a classroom situation, even with a small group of three or four, it's difficult for even the most dedicated teacher to stop all the students over and over in order to demonstrate to one of them how relaxed the shoulders should be, how the hand should hold the bow, where the contact point should be on the strings.

Where are the hips, the elbows, the head and chin and yes, even the belly? Where, before you even lift the bow to play, is every single part of your body?

In fact, the true "instrument" of a violinist begins at the musician's feet—literally, the ground you're standing upon. The sound that comes from the strings reflects not just a performer's musicality, but how well the rest of the body is, or isn't, working. And just as with world-class athletes, the sooner a musician develops the proper form and commits it to body memory, the better the performance will be. In a very real sense, I was out of shape. It was a lesson I never forgot, and today, I'm as adamant about how my students look (even the littlest ones) as I am about how they sound.

Fortunately, I had two teachers at Fredonia who believed in me. Dr. Homer Garretson was my violin teacher; Dr. Lewis Richardson was a cellist. They were the first to explain that each violinist has his or her unique sound, an actual signature. These signatures are as varied as there are human body types and personalities. They told me I had a very special sound; they even said I made a beautiful tone. I had developed a good vibrato and I had accurate intonation—I could pick out a wrong note across the college parking lot. Nevertheless, I would have to work hard to overcome the lack of technical training. This was where I first began to really understand the importance of foundations being built early. Children soak up knowledge like sponges, and the younger they are while they're learning, the greater the advantage they have.

Unlike a lot of young musicians, I already knew I wasn't headed for the Philharmonic or the Met, so hearing that I had a "deficit" in my musicianship didn't send me sobbing to my room. It did, however, set the aspiration bar higher. Even acknowledging that my goal was never to be a "grande artiste" didn't soften the blow of being found less than perfect in what I was doing. Guy Guaspari's daughter falling short of someone's expectations? Falling short of her _own_ expectations? "Just tell me what I have to do to get it right," I pleaded.

So I dug in and the time flew by. There were piano lessons, recital seminars, music theory courses, and classes in conducting. As a music education major, I wasn't required to take many courses not directly pertaining to music—not much in literature, for example, and I never took a language course. I did have one science course, in chemistry, and did very well in it; in fact, the professor suggested that I think about majoring in chemistry. In recent years, as all the research studies of how music affects the brain have hit the headlines, I've begun to realize that my relatively easy success with math and sciences was as attributable to the work I was doing with my violin as it was to whatever skill with numbers I had inherited from my mother.

I took all the electives in art that I could—drawing, painting, and pottery, which reminded me of learning to bake with my mother and grandmother. I liked the way the clay felt in my hands and the way the studio smelled. I especially liked having an object that I had made—a mug, a vase—that I could hold, or look at, or give away. For a while I thought about a minor, possibly even a second major, in studio art. Dr. Garretson, my violin teacher, wisely made me rethink that. Becoming an expert on a musical instrument is a tightly focused endeavor, he cautioned. It involves actually playing that instrument for hours every day, both in class and in practice sessions. True dedication meant there would be no time left to do anything else.

So while the world outside was going through huge changes—the Civil Rights movement, the anti-war demonstrations on college campuses—my own world quietly narrowed down to my violin, the goals I had set, and the practice room in the music department. I decided that after leaving Fredonia, I would need to go on to graduate school for an advanced degree in music education. There was so much more to learn, more to achieve, in order to be as good as I wanted to be. I applied to Boston University and was accepted.

I was quite surprised at the response this news elicited around the family table. *"What?"* exclaimed my grandfather, his arms flying up in the air with alarm. "You gonna go to *more* college?" He looked completely exasperated. "Go, go! Getta' more education—you gonna be'a so smart, *nobody* gonna want you!"

While they had always been proud of me, more school was not on anyone's list of What Roberta Was Supposed to Do Next—not even for my dad. When was I going to find a good man and get going on the part of life that was most important? Besides, they said, B.U. was expensive, maybe even a little elitist; I would be a fish out of water there. Surely I could see that it wasn't such a good idea, couldn't I? But I had made up my mind—and once I did that, it was done.

I wasn't in Boston long before I began to wonder if maybe my family, and specifically my grandfather, had been right. I was as lonely as I had ever been in my life.

Many of my fellow BU students had attended very prestigious music schools or had received more sophisticated training than I had. At that level, we were expected to have studied with famous people, music teachers with national or even international reputations whose names would be instantly recognizable in conversation. In spite of my efforts at Fredonia, my technique was still not as strong as it should have been in that company.

Rather than rising to the challenge, I simply grew more self-conscious about my musicianship with each passing day. I had always loved performing. Now, it only meant greater pressure.

I lived in an apartment complex near Cambridge, and found my roommates through a commercial roommate service, which led to a whole series of odd matches. One girl was perfectly charming and I just knew we would become great friends. Unfortunately, at about the same time I noticed that she always seemed to have a great deal of money, I discovered that she was a prostitute—happily for her, a successful one. Not so happily for me.

And my parents had been right about another thing: Boston was very expensive. The simplest things—the car (I definitely had a lemon), groceries, strings for the violin—seemed to empty my wallet with amazing speed. I got a part-time job as a waitress, which was just about the only job a full-time student can have and still devote any time to course work, which for me included hours of practice.

But I had neglected to take into consideration that in spite of its colonial history and its "Puritan Yankee" culture, Boston was basically a college town, and the people I was waiting on often acted like every day was spring break. Of course, a big part of that behavior was about the changing culture and expectations of the times. The social and sexual attitudes of the sixties were rolling right into the seventies, and there was a sense of great freedom and openness—free form, invent your own rules—that energized a lot of people. It only frightened me.

However, leaving school and going back home—that was never an option. I made decisions, I stuck to them, and I completed things; but, more and more, I asked myself just what I thought I was doing, not just in this city and in this graduate program, but in my life. The path had always seemed so clear to me—achieving the goal, no matter what that was, had always been simply a matter of discipline, focus, and energy. Why wasn't it working this time? Why, I asked myself, am I so damn miserable?

In June of 1971, I had completed my course work and all the requirements for my graduate degree except for my thesis. My plan was to spend the summer in Boston working on it. I had made some friends and finally had begun dating, but there was no one who particularly interested me. And then I met Charles.*

Charles was a distinct improvement over the men I had been meeting up to that point. He was, put simply, an old-fashioned nice guy. Good-looking and clean cut (which in those days made him stand out), Charles was a commissioned officer in the navy, an Annapolis graduate, recently back in the states after a stint in Vietnam. When we met, he was a student at MIT, finishing up his graduate degree in civil engineering, after which he was scheduled to go to Hawaii for a tour of duty. He loved the navy, he told me, and planned to make a career of it.

It took only a couple of dates for me to know that I was in love with this man. He was so gentle, so intelligent and calm—a safe harbor at a time when I'd been feeling restless and unfocused. And unlike a lot of other people I knew at that time, Charles had a life plan. He knew where he was going and precisely how he was going to get there. Almost as important, he had an ethnic background and values similar to mine, although his

---

*To protect the privacy of the individual mentioned here, this name is a pseudonym and will be used throughout the book.

family was Greek and he was an only child. His parents lived in New Jersey; he was their pride and joy, for all the right reasons.

We had been dating for only three weeks when we decided to take off for a weekend, to Newport, Rhode Island, for the music festival. We drove south in his little green Fiat on a beautiful June day, sunny and clear, not one cloud in the blue sky. We spent the afternoon of the concert walking together on the beach, climbing up and down the rocks, holding hands, and getting sunburned. And it was there that Charles asked me to marry him.

Of course it all happened too fast. I didn't know who he was; he didn't know who I was. Maybe, at that age, we weren't actually anybody yet. All I knew was that it was time for me to make this commitment and that this was the person I wanted to make it to. I had let other guys go by, good guys, because I had been waiting for something—but I didn't know what. To be swept away, maybe. For lightning to strike. And what was happening between us felt like lightning to me.

For reasons I can't even remember (if, indeed, I had ever understood what they were), there was a riot at the festival quite early on. It reportedly started when some people climbed over the fences without paying for their tickets. No one in town or affiliated with the concert had anticipated the huge crowd, and very quickly, things went out of control. Emotions ran very high; there was shouting, screaming, fights, and police everywhere. An announcement came over the P.A. system:

"Please exit in an orderly fashion, your lives are in danger." We were surrounded by complete anarchy, total craziness—everything that was going on out in the world that I wanted nothing to do with. The strong arm around my shoulder seemed to be what stood between me and all of that. He would always keep me safe.

By the time Charles got us safely back to the car and out of Newport, it was still relatively early in the evening. I called my parents from the road—we were only four hours or so from Rome, why not just drive all the way up there and introduce them to their future son-in-law? "I'm getting married," I announced giddily. "I'm bringing him up to Rome to meet you, and we have to make plans, because he's going to Hawaii in a few weeks, and I'm going with him."

We drove into my parents' driveway at 2 A.M., but it could have been high noon. The lights were on, everybody was up, the feast was on the table. I had just finished making the first round of family introductions when all of a sudden I noticed the top of my grandmother's curly gray head bobbing along just outside the kitchen window—she was strolling casually past the house, and she was whistling. "Ma," my mother called, "just what are you doing out there? It's two in the morning!"

"Oh, I couldn't sleep, so I thought I would take a little walk," Gramma said, but she didn't fool anybody. She had been watching for the car, eagerly waiting for the chance to inspect the future groom. "Maybe I'll just come in for a few minutes and have something to eat."

She came in, scrutinized Charles (who bore it quite gracefully), and gave us her stamp of approval.

After that, events seemed to take on a life and speed of their own; Charles and I were merely passengers on the train. There had to be a church ceremony of course, but which church—Roman Catholic or Greek Ortho-dox? Our family priest refused to perform an ecumeni-cal service, since we wouldn't sign a pledge to raise our children Catholic. My parents were disappointed—not in me, but in the church doctrine.

I was gratified when they agreed to a Greek Ortho-dox wedding, to be performed by a friend of Charles's family, Father John, who would come up from New Jer-sey to perform the ceremony. Although I certainly couldn't claim to have been a theological scholar, I didn't see any contradictory differences between the two religions—to me, they looked like two "wings" of the same house—and so I had little trouble, a few months after the wedding, deciding to convert to Charles's faith. It seemed like the right thing to do, part of the vows I was making to join my life to his.

The wedding was held at the military chapel at Grif-fiss Air Force Base in Rome, three months after we'd first met. Charles wore his white uniform, we cut the wedding cake with his sword, and went off to the Ca-ribbean on a brief honeymoon. "Now I can sleep," my dad said as my parents went to bed that night. "Roberta is going to be all right."

In the beginning, we lived in an apartment in the city of Honolulu; two years later we would move to Wahiawa, a small town near Oahu's North Shore, surrounded by pineapple fields and sugarcane. For the first few weeks, I awoke each day in a world I couldn't quite believe: new marriage, new home, new life, on a tropical island in the middle of the Pacific. When I looked out the window, I could see actual coconut trees.

I had a thesis to finish, so I began the process of dealing with my B.U. advisors by mail. I had my violin, of course, and I practiced every day, drawing comfort from the feel of the instrument in my hands and the sound of the music I could make. I also had my schnauzer, Duffy, but he was in quarantine for four months. I visited him in the kennel as often as I could, but I knew I couldn't center my days around chatting with a dog and waiting for my husband to come home from work.

At first, teaching possibilities looked slim. The first strike against me (and this would follow me around for many years) was being a military wife. Employers are understandably reluctant to invest any time or attention in someone they know will just move away in two or three years.

I did manage to talk my way into a gift-wrapping job with a clothing store during the holiday season—and within days, I was summarily fired! I was over-qualified, they said, which was a polite way of saying what they really meant: My insistence on coordinating the perfect wrapping paper with the most intricately and beautifully tied bow made me much too slow to be of any use to anyone during a rushed buying season.

It was a humbling experience, as was my audition for a position with the Honolulu Symphony. I didn't get the job—I simply wasn't prepared in the right way for an audition like that, and my nerves got the best of me. Chastened, I visited a small Suzuki school about an hour away to investigate teaching possibilities and hear the kids play in a concert. I had already done a great deal of research on the Suzuki method in preparation for writing my thesis. While there were no teaching positions, what I saw and heard there influenced my thinking about teaching kids to play music in a way nothing had before.

The Suzuki method was begun in Japan by Shinichi Suzuki, and its introduction in the United States caused educators to completely rethink the way children learn to play an instrument. With Suzuki, kids begin very early—in some cases as young as three—with tiny, one-tenth-size violins, and they learn a fixed repertory, one selection at a time, in order of increasing difficulty. There's a lot of repetition, and the kids learn each piece by heart—learning to read music comes much later, after they've developed some familiarity with the instrument and some confidence in themselves.

In the Suzuki method, parental involvement and home practice are of key importance; in a very real way, the teacher and the parents are equal partners. There are numerous wonderful examples of Suzuki success, but in recent years it has come up against a number of walls—the parental side of the partnership has become much harder to arrange, given the rise in single-parent homes and the reality that one or both parents are holding down full-time jobs.

In any case, that Suzuki concert was a revelation for me for two major reasons. First, I was struck by how many of the violinists were so little: tiny young children, who would have seemed perfectly at home stacking alphabet building blocks in a nursery school. Yet they all were making real music. This wasn't a room full of so-called gifted kids, preselected for this training by some kind of specialized intelligence test. These were just ordinary children, busily proving Suzuki's hypothesis that all children can learn to play the violin just as easily (and just as early) as they learn their mother language. Second, the group of young violinists was my first real introduction to the blend of the culture, language, and ethnic heritage found in the Islands. Polynesian, Samoan, Chinese, Japanese, Portuguese, African-American, and *haole* (white) kids, all playing beautifully together, conducted and taught by a black man named Charles Wellington. *This is the ideal of what teaching, and music, can be*, I thought. It represented everything I wanted to do.

That's not to say that everything was perfect in paradise: The Hawaiian secession-from-America movement was beginning, and occasionally we would hear about a group of high-school students discussing "Kill Haole Day" in their school. It was a time of great transition in

Hawaii, and a challenging time for me to begin my career teaching music in the public schools.

In January I was offered a general music teaching position at Wheeler Intermediate School (on Wheeler Air Force base). While at Wheeler I met Rainie Smith, another music teacher. I had no way of knowing then that Rainie would become one of my lifelong friends. I only knew that I had met a kindred spirit. She was a gifted musician, choreographer, director, and conductor—and had an amazing impact on her students. She was crazy about them, and they knew it. She simply convinced them that they could do anything. Even the most difficult, challenging kids got caught up in her energy and enthusiasm. At one point she had a group of huge Samoan high-school boys (who would have been more at home on the football field) harmonizing to Handel and dancing to Broadway show music.

Rainie's husband was in the military, too, although he was an enlisted man. I didn't know at that point that it was frowned upon for officers—and their wives—to spend a great deal of time with enlisted friends, but I would hear about it soon enough. In fact, I was slowly beginning to comprehend that I had two identities: first, the one inside my own four walls, where I lived with my husband and we learned a little more about each other every day; second, the one outside, where I was a navy wife. Out there, my existence was completely overshadowed by Charles's position. His military rank, as indicated by the official sticker on our car, earned me a sharp salute every time I drove through the gate at the base, even when I was alone in the car. The first time it happened (the guard called me "ma'am" as he saluted me through), I did a double take. I thought it was some kind of funny mistake—a case of mistaken identity, maybe.

"No," Charles told me. "That's what they're supposed to do. It's a mark of respect for the rank."

"But I'm not in the navy," I said.

He smiled gently. "Oh, yes, Bobbi, you are."

Love Knows Not Its Depth

Shortly after Charles and I arrived in Hawaii, I made an appointment with my new doctor to get a physical exam—my very first Pap smear—and to discuss birth control. A few days later, I received a disturbing phone call from the doctor's office. The test had revealed the existence of some kind of abnormal cell growth, possibly cancerous.

Another appointment and more tests left us with a diagnosis of severe cervical dysplasia. The prognosis, the doctor said, might mean anything from not being able to conceive children to the need for a complete hysterectomy.

I was stunned and scared, and so was my husband.

Although we were going to wait for a while before having children (after all, we had only known each other a few months), the idea that we might never have them at all had simply never occurred to us. And now, not even a possible threat to my own health was as devastating as the possibility of not having babies.

We began a nerve-wracking regimen of more tests, biopsies, and tissue removals every six weeks, for the better part of the following year. The doctors didn't want us to be physically intimate during this time, which only added to the stress and my loneliness. At a time when Charles and I most needed to be close to each other (and would have been, given the newness of the marriage), we were instead often restrained and almost cautious with each other.

With each round of treatment, my fear and anxiety increased. I'd start agonizing the night before and wouldn't be able to sleep. For some reason, the procedures brought back vivid memories of my childhood catechism sessions at St. John the Baptist Church. The soul could be ruined by mortal sin, the nuns taught us, but it was only smudged by venial sin. Through confession, however, those imperfections are erased and the soul is restored to health again. Every time the doctors removed more cervical tissue, I pictured a soul—for some reason, I always saw it as round and white—and the smudgy part was being removed. And when they were finished, I wondered, would the soul indeed be restored to health?

After the treatments were finally over, the doctors

weren't willing—or able—to answer our question about having a child. Maybe, maybe not—but given the presence of so much scar tissue, they doubted it. "You better start trying to get pregnant now," they said, "because we don't know what will happen down the road." To maximize my chances, they put me on a course of fertility drugs.

Almost immediately, my emotions starting going up and down in contrary motion with my hormone level. One day I ate everything in the kitchen; the next day I was perfectly satisfied with diet soda and an apple. I could easily gain ten pounds in ten days, and then just as easily lose them. As my moods raged from one end of the house to the other, so did my body temperature. I was hot, I was cold, and I was desperately homesick. Poor Charles, who was doing his best to put up with the crazy woman his wife had become, alternated between quiet support and complete exasperation. This was not what he had imagined the day he proposed to me on the beach.

After two and a half years of illness, treatment, scar tissue, and roller coaster hormones, I didn't have much hope left. Rainie's family had moved into the apartment right next to ours, and we even shared the same car port. Her daughter Rachel was about three then, and almost every day I watched the two of them with longing, the little girl clinging happily to her mother's hand, and I wondered if I would ever have what they had. And then, suddenly, it happened. I was pregnant.

I couldn't believe it; I almost felt guilty at having

doubted. The wave of joy I felt when the pregnancy was actually confirmed overwhelmed me, the emotion was so much larger than anything I had ever experienced. Suddenly, all the music I had ever heard and all the music I had ever played seemed to make the most perfect sense. Charles, too, was ecstatic—we used the word *miracle* a lot. And back in New York and New Jersey, of course, four future grandparents were happily losing their minds.

With all the medical and reproductive drama, my teaching career had gotten off to a bumpy start. I had been moved around Oahu's public schools quite a bit—from general music teacher at Wheeler to choral director of the Radford High School Regalaires to Mauna Loa Intermediate School, where I taught string classes (viola, violin, cello and bass, all at once) and directed the chorus and full orchestra.

Soon after the 1974–75 school year began, I was finally beginning to feel at home at Mauna Loa, as I rejoiced in my pregnancy and started to work with my students on the preparations for our holiday concert. Although I'd had very little choral training myself, I was getting tips from Rainie, who collaborated with me in the evenings. Soon enough, the program we came up with was so much fun, the kids were willingly giving up lunch hours and staying after school to rehearse. They were singing Coltrane jazz, the "Hallelujah Chorus" from Handel's *Messiah*, and selections from *Godspell* in glorious three-part harmony.

In every way, the excitement and joy the kids were feeling reflected my own. My energy flowed into them; theirs flowed back to me—it was the open circuit. At twenty-six, with hair all the way down to my waist and wearing my ever-expanding "hippie" smock dresses and brightly flowered Hawaiian muumuus, I looked like one of the kids myself, just quite a bit rounder. As the baby began to move and kick—and the kids began to notice— the pregnancy felt like a class project, almost on a par with the concert itself.

On the night of December 15, I stayed up long past midnight, baking. For days I had been making dozens of traditional Greek *koulourakia* and Italian Christmas cookies to give to our friends as gifts, in the same way my mother had done, complete with the multicolored icings. After the baking itself, I would arrange each tray as though it was a piece of art, with the right colors and textures next to each other, all tied off with holiday ribbon.

On this particular night, when I mixed the colors for the last batch of frosting, I goofed: It turned a garish shade of purple. That had been my last box of confectioner's sugar—it was too late to send Charles out for another one, too late to start all over again. Of course, any rational person would've said it was too late for me to be up at all, but that wasn't the point. In any case, I completely fell apart. I cried and cried. My legs hurt, my shoulders hurt. Charles tried his best to comfort me, but I paid no attention. "I can't give purple cookies for Christmas!" I sobbed. Finally, exhausted, we went to bed.

The following day at school, sleep-deprived and puffy, I was in the middle of a chorus rehearsal when a student came into the band room with a note for me. It was from the principal, asking me to come to his office immediately. The word *immediately* jumped right off the paper. It was a few minutes walk across campus to his office; as I walked, I began to feel more and more nervous. What had I done? What was wrong?

When I got to the office, I was surprised to see Charles, in his uniform, standing rigidly next to the principal's desk. His face was so pale and his expression so tense that I was terrified before he said a word. "Who is it?" I exclaimed, my voice rising. "Is it my mother?"

"It's your father," he said, and then he looked away. I felt my legs give way beneath me.

At the Revere factory, it had always been the custom for the company to hire local kids (whose parents were also employed at the factory) to work in the summers and during the holidays to earn extra money for college. My dad—the rules man, the perfectionist, the safety fanatic—had been called into work that day to fix a furnace that had broken down. While he was inside the furnace, one of these kids, not understanding the tagging system (which would have told him there was someone in there), started up a huge piston—a machine at least a half a block long. My dad shouted, and they tried to shut it down, but the piston had gathered too much momentum. It was too late. In seconds, he was crushed; in minutes, he was dead.

The message my father had left on his blackboard that week was from Kahlil Gibran's *The Prophet*: "Love knows not its depth until the hour of separation."

My obstetrician strongly suggested that I not get on a plane and fly home. The trip, with the necessary connections and possible delays, could take anywhere from ten to twenty hours, and the stress could easily bring on premature labor. The baby's lungs weren't developed, and my own health would be at risk as well.

Charles and I talked and talked. To think that only the night before, I was sobbing over purple frosting— and at that very moment, my father was still alive, still in my life. Why had I thrown such a ridiculous scene, why had I made myself sick over something that was so unimportant compared to the pain and loss I was feeling right now?

Rainie and I went for a long walk on the beach, holding hands as she comforted me, trying to help me make my decision. Afterwards, Charles drove me up to our little Greek church on the Pali mountain range so I could speak with our priest. The phone rang incessantly with calls from friends at church and school, and from my family, now so unbelievably far away. How could I not be with them? How could I balance the safety of my baby with saying good-bye to the father I adored?

And what about the Christmas concert, and all those kids who had worked so hard? They were told when I left school that my father had been killed in an accident in New York; I'm sure they assumed that I would have to go home. In fact, the principal told them that he thought the concert would be canceled.

Gradually, it became apparent in the words I was hearing all around me and in the message I heard deep inside my heart that what my dad would have wanted was for the well-being of his grandchild to come first. Besides, I knew I couldn't let the kids down. After all, my dad was the one who had wanted me to be a teacher in the first place.

So I didn't go home—I stayed in Hawaii. On the very day my father was being buried in Rome, we dedicated our concert to his memory and in his honor.

There is no way to convey what those kids gave to me that day—the sheer beauty of their orchestral playing, the purity of their voices. They really did sound like angels. The child inside me pushed and kicked. I felt like my dad was right there with us—or we were somehow with him. No Christmas mass (or funeral) could have given me what those kids gave me in terms of solace and spiritual strength, which came rolling back to me with each note. I stood strong because of the sound they made; it sustained me for weeks, through the sadness that lingered during Christmas and into the New Year, and then into the spring.

Nicholas Guy, named after his paternal grandfather and my dad, was born on March 28. It was Good Friday. It was also my father's birthday.

When Nick was nine months old, Charles was transferred to Newport, Rhode Island. Although the years in Hawaii had been bittersweet, I felt a tinge of regret to leave the beauty of it behind. In Rhode Island, though, we would be closer to our families, and Nick would learn what it was to be part of something so much larger than just his father and mother.

We bought a lovely house near the Sakonnet River in Tiverton, one of the historic coastal communities. There was a freestanding brick fireplace in the center of the open-beamed living room, and a long front deck that overlooked the river. Eagerly, I set about making another home.

Given how difficult it had been to conceive our first child, we had no idea if I would be able to have another, or how long it might take to get pregnant. When Nick was a year old, I stopped using birth control; surprisingly, our second child (a son who would be named Alexi) was conceived immediately.

If the navy ran true to form, I knew we would probably be in Rhode Island for only a couple of years. Between caring for one baby and being pregnant with another, it didn't seem the right time for me to look for a job teaching music. Instead, we bought a pottery wheel and kiln, and I began throwing pots, both as an outlet for my own need to create art and as a way to earn some money—because I always felt that I had to make up for money that I spent on anything Charles classified as "not practical." The wheel and kiln cost a little over a thousand dollars. Charles, who kept the books, wasn't thrilled about the expenditure. He made all the decisions about our money, and he was conservative with it. He paid all the bills; I never saw them. My paychecks for teaching (and for whatever pottery I sold) were always immediately endorsed and went right into the bank. To his credit, though, he tried to get involved in pottery with me—he learned to glaze, and even made his own chemical recipes for glazes.

We often traveled around to various crafts shows and fairs, curious about the kind of work other artists did, and trying to sell our own. One day I drove past a beautiful French restaurant—it was actually a huge renovated barn—with skylights and big windows, and trees that were growing inside. When I went in, I discovered that not only did Bernard's Café in the Barn have a gift shop that sold crafts and pottery, they also used musicians to entertain their guests. "I'm a violinist," I said. Could they use me? Yes, they could.

At first I only played during lunch in the early afternoon, perched on a stool with my violin. Then I began playing on weekends for the dinner crowd. The restaurant owner paid me twenty-five or thirty dollars each session, and afterward always made sure I sat down and enjoyed a delicious four-course French meal. As time passed, I began to know and recognize the regular customers, some of whom seemed to be coming back, not just for the wonderful food and service, but to see how big the pregnant violinist was getting. And I was getting *huge*. By the end of all this wining and dining, I had put on seventy pounds—only six and a half pounds of that would ultimately be Alexi!

Between the music and the pottery I sold at the restaurant and the crafts festivals, I easily paid back the money for the wheel and the kiln. I kept enough pots to have hanging plants all over our house.

I was busy with other things, too. I was building a relationship with Yaya and Papu (Greek for grandparents), Charles's parents in New Jersey. I was learning some Greek phrases and had become quite proficient at cooking and baking the traditional food. On Sundays, Charles and I went to the Greek Orthodox church in Fall River, where I taught Sunday school.

During mass, the youngest children, including little Nick, would be downstairs with me. We would all come back up again a few minutes before Communion was given, just as the priest was about to sing the consecration. In the Orthodox tradition, he sings the phrase in Greek three times, the first two in exactly the same way. For the third repetition, the harmonic resolution of the cadence resolves differently, which reflects the transformation of the bread and wine. As he sings the last words, the priest raises his hands in a gesture of rejoicing.

One October day before Alexi was born, Charles and I decided to take a drive to see the leaves; the foliage season in Rhode Island is truly magnificent. As we drove, we were lulled by the peace and beauty just outside the windows. Nick, about eighteen months old, was tucked into the infant seat. We had been driving for a little while when all of a sudden, from the backseat, came the baby voice of my son, singing—verbatim—the consecration phrases from the mass. In perfect Greek and in tune. He ended the recital by raising his chubby little arms straight up to the roof of the car. We were stunned. "A musician," I said. "That baby's a natural musician!"

When Nick was two and a half and Alexi was eight months old, Charles was transferred to Greece. Our new home was in Nea Makri, a coastal village just twenty-six miles from Athens on the Marathon Run. Rather than live up over the mountain in Kiffisia, a wealthy suburb where all the other officers' families lived, we found a large but modest house near the beach. In my memory I can still see the terrazzo floors, the veranda that ran around the entire house, the long-stemmed roses that grew like sunflowers, and the boys' swing set out in the yard.

In Greece, everyone thought that I was the Greek

one, not Charles. Although he could understand the language better than I, he was reluctant at first to speak it. I carried the *Conversational Greek* phonics book everywhere I went—it actually had been written by his uncle and given to me by his parents. I studied its pages constantly, pronouncing the words and phrases out loud whenever I could. One of Nick's first full sentences was, "Oh, no, Mommy, please, not the Greek book!"

Nea Makri was an easy drive from Athens, and many people from the city had second homes near the water. All along the rocky shore there were little rundown tavernas that did a booming business all day, serving fresh calamari, *spiti retsina* (the pungent house wine flavored with pine resin), and *horiatiko salatas*—big country salads with fresh vegetables, Greek olives, and feta cheese.

During the summer, the beach, only a half block down our dirt road, was crowded and busy. During the winter, however, there was almost no one around. Every morning, I would walk Nick and Lexi down to what we soon called "Nicky's beach," where the women from the village were gathered with their own children. In Greece, baby boys are treated like gifts directly from God, and I had two of them. Although the women spoke no English, my diligence with the Greek book paid off— slowly, the language barrier disappeared. Laughing, they helped me with my bad pronunciation and flawed grammar as I tried to make myself understood by using exaggerated charades gestures and waving my hands in the air like the true granddaughter of Giuseppe Vitali. In a few weeks, we were having real conversations—

about children, food, and what life was like in America. In many ways, it was as much fun for me as playing chamber music with a group of my favorite musicians.

Charles, now the public works officer on the base, loved his job. His career was obviously on a good track; the more responsibility they gave him, the more he seemed to thrive, and the more committed he was to making a lifetime career of the navy.

I was always an integral part of my husband's fitness reports, and I suspect I was "written up" as a mixed asset. It was a great advantage that I spoke the language and understood the culture, and was always willing to be an ambassador between the local people and the military, as well as a liaison with the enlisted families. I tended to gravitate toward the enlisted wives anyway—our children were close in age, and in terms of my own age (I had just turned 30) and experience, I had more in common with them than I did with the officers' wives, whose kids were mostly in high school.

I went to a Greek language class that was held on the base, and there I met a woman named Evie, who taught high school French and Spanish at The American School. Her husband was a navy chief (an enlisted rank), and her son was just a year older than Nick. We connected immediately and became close friends. She didn't have much tolerance for stuffiness (we giggled a lot, in the same way I had done with Rainie), and we bonded over the things we had in common.

However, friendship between the enlisted and the officers was frowned upon—it was called fraternization, and it was against the rules. After Evie's car had been seen too many times in our driveway, Charles got the word from someone superior to him. His wife was going over the line, and he needed to step in and do something about that.

I understood the need for rank and rules—there are ranks and rules in music, too—and certainly I wanted to do whatever I could to support my husband's career. But in this particular case, I felt that the rules made little sense, and I said as much to my husband. Someone told me the no-fraternization rule had something to do with morale—but how could putting up barriers between potential friends be a morale builder? After all, we were all Americans and we were all a long way from home. Why make that harder than it already was?

For the enlisted personnel, life was already pretty hard, certainly harder than it was for officers and their families. Many of them were quite young, barely out of high school. The salary at the lowest ranks did not provide for dependents; if they were married, they had to make the hard choice of either leaving their families in the states for two or three years or bringing them overseas and struggling with the poverty that made many of them eligible for food stamps. Most of them didn't speak any Greek, which further increased their isolation. Even in that beautiful setting there was often a great deal of tension, both in the relations with the Greek community and behind the closed doors of the enlisted families.

So although I was warned against it, I kept up my

friendship with Evie. When we wanted to see each other, we simply drove separately to Marathon, the next town over, where we would meet and take our kids to the beach for the afternoon. I didn't do it to be difficult or rebellious, or to make life difficult for my husband. I did it because I didn't think the navy had the right to choose my friends for me. Sometimes, I thought, strict adherence to rules is just an excuse not to have to think for yourself.

The spring after we arrived in Greece, I auditioned for the National Symphony Orchestra in Athens. This time, I was ready for the stress and the scrutiny—but my timing was bad. The audition coincided with a strike; an American taking a striker's job would have been, politically, a very bad idea.

That summer, Charles and I met a wealthy couple whose country home (a couple of beautiful acres tumbling down to the water) was just down the block from our house. Demetrias and Eleni had a little boy, Stephanos, who was exactly Nick's age. Eleni told me about Campion, a private British school that Stephanos was attending. It was in a small town just over the mountain from Nea Makri. "Why don't you go and investigate it?" she said. "Nick could probably go to Campion—and maybe you could even teach there."

When I went to the school, I discovered that while they had a perfectly fine music department, the violin instruction was limited to the kids at the high-school level. However, they were very interested in having me teach and asked if I wanted to set up a violin program for the younger children. The only problem, they said, was that they didn't have any violins.

It started me thinking. Charles was a career officer. I was his dependent, and by definition, we were transient. I was probably going to move to a new community every two or three years for the rest of my life, and every time, I would face this same scenario: No matter how well I taught or how great my references were, potential employers would always be reluctant to hire me. In addition, military families often find themselves in cultures where Americans aren't particularly welcome or where attitudes toward women make it hard for them to be accepted (or even allowed) to get jobs in local communities. Clearly, if I wanted to continue to teach children to play the violin, no matter where we lived, no matter how rich or poor those children were, I could not rely on any existing program—I had to find a way to make my *own* program and carry it with me. So I went to Charles with a proposition: "I want to buy a bunch of violins."

I figured this would address both the immediate problem and the long-term one—I could ask for a per diem salary from Campion, the parents could rent the instruments from me for the year, and when we moved, the violins would move with us. No matter what happened, kids could always have violins and I would always have a job.

Charles readily agreed—but how many should we

buy? To gauge potential interest, Campion School sent out a questionnaire asking parents if they would be interested in having their younger children take violin lessons. Seventy families replied with an enthusiastic yes; of those, twenty kids had their own violins.

Together, Charles and I drove into Athens in our camper and began to shop around in the small mom-and-pop businesses tucked into every side street and alley in the city. In Greece, though, you don't actually shop, you bargain—and I had learned my bargaining skills from the world's best, my mother. "How much will you take for a violin?" I asked. "OK, how about if I buy ten? How about if I buy twenty? What about fifty?"

In the end we spent $5,000. We went home with a camper full of fifty violins, all sizes, complete with bows, cases, and plenty of extra rosin and string. They were poorly made little things. I worried that we had paid much more than we should have. I had no way of knowing that in the long run, those violins would prove to be worth every drachma.

Blinded

*O*ur life in Nea Makri soon fell into a lovely rhythm, with one sun-warmed day after another occupied with work we both enjoyed and two little boys we adored, plus new friends, great food, and plenty of music. In that setting, the beauty and abundance of nature was everywhere around us, and it was easy to bask in its glory.

The pottery wheel and kiln were put to good use—I made all the dishes we ate on, as well as the serving platters and many vases of every conceivable size and color. We entertained a great deal—dinner parties for twelve, everyone gathered around our long teak dining room table. I planned each gathering as though it was an event somewhere between a military operation and a theatrical production, sketching out each detail, deciding on the menu, gathering the ingredients, and cooking everything from scratch. There were candles everywhere, and cut flowers from our garden on the table, on the windowsills, even on the kitchen counter. Often after dinner, someone asked me to play my violin.

Even Nick, who went to Campion with me on my teaching days, was learning to play, on a tiny, one-tenth-size violin. And I was learning, from him and my other students, that little ones take a great deal on faith: If the teacher tells them that they're capable of doing something, why then, they simply do it. One day I would watch a student struggle to figure out how to hold a violin; soon enough, I would see the grin of delight as he heard himself actually making music on it.

Alexi, still a toddler, was cared for by Matina, a woman from the village who had three teenage daughters who spoiled him rotten. Both boys were soaking up their Greek heritage and learning the language of their grandparents with enviable ease. During our vacations, we put hundreds of miles on the camper as we took the kids and explored Greece, Spain, Italy, Switzerland, France, England, and Holland.

And so, although I thought I had come to terms with the transient status that is a necessary ingredient in military life, I was understandably saddened when Charles was notified after three years that it was time for us to be moving on, this time back to the states. He was to be the commanding officer of a mobile construction unit based in Port Hueneme, California, although in reality he would be alternating between the island of Guam and Rota, Spain—eight months out, six months back home, eight months out again.

It wasn't just leaving Greece that concerned me. This time, Charles wouldn't be allowed to take his dependents with him. The boys and I would live in California, in what I was told was a lovely house on the base. Port Hueneme was a coastal town, as Nea Makri was—surely we wouldn't have a problem with making the transition from one ocean to another. Would we?

I tried to imagine what it would be like, with Charles away from us for long stretches of time. I would have sole responsibility for the boys in an unfamiliar place, and their daddy wouldn't be around much. From the time they were infants, he had been a hands-on father—unlike a lot of dads at that time, he wasn't ever reluctant to change diapers or give them a bottle; in fact, he happily and willingly took on more than his share of midnight feedings, and was just as likely to get up with them at night as I was. I didn't want him to become a stranger to his sons, which I knew happened sometimes in military families. Well, I thought, I'll just have to work hard to see that it doesn't happen to us. And then I began to pack.

During our final six weeks in Greece, we were moved out of our house and into a small hotel overlooking the beach. Our belongings had all been loaded onto the container ship that would go back to the states ahead of us. Before we could actually head for California, Charles had to first deal with a number of military-related appointments on the East Coast in preparation for his new assignment. We planned to build a vacation around his business schedule, first spending a couple of weeks with Yaya and Papu in New Jersey, then taking the boys up to Rome to visit with my family.

The day before we were to leave, while Charles was wrapping up the final details in his office, the boys and I spent the afternoon on the beach that we had grown to love. Determined to put the best face on this move that I possibly could, I chatted comfortably with a German couple for awhile, bragging about my beautiful sons, my wonderful husband, and this interesting life we had that was allowing us to see so much of the world.

That night at the hotel, I repacked our suitcases as the boys slept, going carefully down the list of preparations for the next morning's plane flight. It would be a long day for all of us, but especially for the little ones. I wanted to make sure we had easy access to coloring books, crayons, and snacks. In the meantime, Charles took Duffy the schnauzer out for a last walk.

Duffy was probably going to be an unhappy dog the next day; he would spend the entire flight down in the cargo compartment surrounded by luggage, huddled in the little wooden traveling "house" that my dad had built for him years before. It had a perfect little dog-size door with his name in calligraphy above it, but I knew he wouldn't take any comfort in that.

It was past midnight when Charles and the dog went out, and I was a little taken aback an hour or so later when I glanced up at the clock and realized he wasn't back yet. There was a full moon on the water, which made it almost as bright as day outside—maybe, I thought, he's savoring these last few minutes in the same way I had done on the beach that afternoon.

By 2 A.M., I had gone from feeling uneasy to being frightened. He had been gone too long—maybe he had been hurt somehow. I couldn't just sit there and wait. Quickly checking on the sleeping boys, I went downstairs to the hotel lobby and spoke anxiously to the man behind the desk. He had been watching us go in and out for weeks; he knew who everyone was. "Have you seen my husband?" I asked in Greek.

Yes, he nodded. "He is with the wife of your friend," he said. "He goes for a walk with her every night."

On some level the man's words made a kind of sense, but somehow their meaning didn't translate. The wife of my friend? Maybe I wasn't as good with Greek as I thought. I turned and went out through the hotel doors, intending to trace Charles's dog-walking route. Inside me, there was a growing feeling that something—I didn't know what—was terribly wrong. I started walking faster and faster, then broke into a run as I neared the beach.

As I ran, I could see, maybe fifty or sixty yards ahead

of me, a couple locked in an embrace. The moon was like a spotlight above their heads, and it cast a big golden swath of light out onto the water behind them. One of them was holding onto a leash. At the end of that leash, silhouetted very clearly in the moonlight, was the little square head and body of a dog. A schnauzer.

I ran and ran, right at them. It was like one of those slow-motion shots in the movies. I could feel my feet lifting, hitting the ground, lifting again, and I could hear my heart pounding in my ears. I'm not sure exactly when I started crying. "What are you doing?" I shouted.

They broke apart when they heard me, and turned, almost in the same kind of movie slow motion. As I reached them I stumbled, and grabbed for my husband's arm. "Bobbi," Charles said. "Bobbi." His voice held only mild surprise.

Of course I recognized the woman immediately. She and her husband, both in the navy, had been in the hotel for the entire time we were there, preparing to be transferred out at the same time. For weeks, in fact, we had regularly socialized with them. We went swimming with them, and we picnicked with them on the beach, where they played with my children. We had eaten dinner with them on the little village square almost every night, and gone out Greek dancing afterward, drinking retsina, enjoying our last few nights in Nea Makri.

I saw Charles and the woman exchange a quick look; in it was a whole world of emotion and information that seemed totally incomprehensible to me.

She said nothing, and stayed where she was. He

shifted the dog's leash from one hand to the other, firmly took hold of my arm, and steered me back toward the hotel. I cried all the way, and he continued murmuring quietly, shushing me, in much the same way he would have if he'd been comforting Nick or Alexi after a tumble and a skinned knee. "OK, Bobbi, OK," he kept saying.

Once we reached our room, I tried to stop crying, but it was no use. "But, Charles, what does this mean?" I asked, hearing my voice get loud. "What are we going to do?"

He shook his head, his face almost expressionless. "I don't know," he said. "I don't know what I want to do with the rest of my life."

I thought my heart would beat its way out of my chest. What on earth was he talking about? We were supposed to be on a plane, with our children, early the next morning—in just a few hours, as a matter of fact. How could he not know what he wanted to do with his life?

"You can't mean that!" I said, shouting now, and quite certain people could hear me out on the street. But I didn't care. I only cared if *he* heard me. "You're my husband, you're Nick and Lexi's dad. I can't believe you're doing this to us. To me." We had been trying to conceive another child. Didn't that matter?

No, it didn't. Without once raising his voice, without ever coming close to breaking down, Charles did not give in to the level of emotion I had reached. Everything was different now, he said calmly. He had been wanting to tell me but didn't know how, so maybe the way it had happened tonight was the best thing for all of us. He didn't know what he wanted to do; he didn't know where he wanted to be; he only knew he wanted to go. And wherever it was, it wasn't going to be with me.

The moon went down, the sun came up, and neither of us slept. And when the time came—with Nick clinging to his father's leg and sobbing, "Don't go, Daddy! Mommy, stop him, don't let him go without us!"—a determined Charles left for the airport and the scheduled flight home.

There was no way I could bring myself to go with him at that point—nauseated with fear and disbelief, I could barely stand upright. And I could not believe he would leave the country without us. But he did.

I spent the next three days in bed in the hotel room, crying.

Of course the word got out in a matter of hours— the scene in the hotel quickly made the gossip network between Nea Makri and the base, and Charles's solo departure did not escape notice. Kind friends took the boys away from the hotel for a couple of days while I lay there and watched the ceiling spin. It was as though I had been hit with a bullet tipped with some kind of narcotic.

My body felt numb, alien somehow, not attached. It reminded me of the *Twilight Zone* episodes I had watched as a child. It was a real nightmare, but I wasn't sure if it was mine. Maybe it was someone else's nightmare and I was just watching it, from somewhere far away. But if it wasn't mine, why couldn't I wake up?

When my father was killed in the factory accident, as heartbreaking as that was for me, there had been no choice for me but to believe it, to accept it, to think of how to move on without him. But this was completely different; on some level, it was even worse. Overnight, the very foundation of my life had crumbled, and nothing I believed in was true. How long, I wondered, had that been the case?

My husband didn't want me. I had no house, no home. Where was I supposed to live with my children? What was I supposed to do next? I had no way to even begin to figure it out. And everything I owned—clothes, dishes, linens, violins, pottery wheel, kiln—was deep in the hold of a ship somewhere between the Mediterranean and California. I felt betrayed, and terrified. And stupid. I hadn't seen any of it coming. If there had been any clues, I missed them.

Slowly, however, fragment by fragment, some things did begin to make a bizarre kind of sense. There were scenes from the past few weeks that now took on an entirely different light. Remembering them, picturing them, made me sick to my stomach.

For instance, one night there had been a heated discussion about the whole fraternization issue, about my continuing friendship with Evie and other enlisted wives. That kind of behavior could have a bad effect on his fitness report, the woman had said, in the kind of voice an adult might use to chide, even scold, a stubborn child. An officer's wife is a vital part of the package, she said. It's possible my husband could go all the way to the top of the ranks—unless I screwed it up.

It had been a thoroughly unpleasant scene, but hardly a catfight. At the time, I dismissed it as a difference of opinion. After all, she wore a uniform, too—it was only natural that she would see things from the navy's side. Only now did I realize I had completely misunderstood her agenda.

And there were a couple of other things as well. There was Charles's recent enthusiasm for Greek dancing on those nights when the four of us went out together. And yes, he had been more animated lately, more carefree, more willing to do things he hadn't wanted to do before—swim in the ocean at night, dance far into the late hours. If anything, that had only contributed to my sense that I was in the middle of a happy marriage. In fact, I had been having a lot of fun.

The woman was tall, model-thin, and in command of her surroundings; I was shorter, with more curves, and all over the place with my emotions and opinions. My husband had joked over the years that if I ever put on weight like my grandmother, he would leave me. But I had lost all the weight I gained with my last pregnancy, and more besides. Maybe it hadn't been enough, I thought.

It took a few days, but finally I psyched myself up to the point where I thought I could trust my voice. I placed a long-distance call to Charles's parents' house in New Jersey. When he came to the phone, I focused as hard as I could on what I had rehearsed, took a deep breath, and began to try and change his mind. I had given it a lot of thought, I said—yes, we clearly had some problems, and what had happened had been awful, but I could forgive him. We had a family, we had a marriage. We could work this out. "Please," I said.

"There's nothing to work out," he answered. It was the same even, distant tone he had used on the beach and in the hotel.

"Charles, no matter what our problems are, I'm willing to do whatever we have to do to solve them," I said passionately. "We can go to marriage counseling. I can change."

"Bobbi, this isn't about you changing," he said quietly. "This is about me and what I want." And what he didn't want anymore was me.

I knew I couldn't stay curled up in a hotel bed forever. I had to get back on my feet, be a mother, prepare to leave Greece—but the thought of getting myself, the boys, and the dog to the airport and on a flight home made me dizzy. There was certainly nothing left for me in Nea Makri. There was no question of staying on, of keeping my teaching job or remaking a life here. The person whose dependent I was had left the country; I had to go, too.

In my memory, the airport seemed very dark once we got there. I remember some kind of confusion about suitcases and the dog's traveling box. The boys, three and five at that point, were wound up like little spring-loaded toys—their dad had left them behind, their mother was completely spaced out. A pediatrician friend gave me a prescription for them to take so they could settle down for the long flight. Unfortunately, I made the mistake of giving the medicine to the boys before we got to the airport, and then discovered that our flight had been delayed for several hours. Long before we were on the plane, the medication wore off, and they just seemed to ricochet all over the place like balls on a pool table. I saw it through a kind of haze. I knew I should probably do something, but what? Kids take their cues from their parents. I was lost, and my two boys knew it.

Charles picked us up at Kennedy Airport. I had expected—I had hoped—that when he actually saw the three of us, he would be somehow softened, relieved that we were safe and all together again. As we loaded the exhausted little boys into the car and started the hour-long drive to my in-laws' home, I kept watching my husband for some positive sign, but there was nothing.

I stayed at his parents' only a day or two. The situation was impossible, and Yaya and Papu were caught squarely in the middle of it. They desperately didn't want to take sides, and the resulting tense silences were like angry storm clouds rolling toward their house. Papu shook his head sadly. "Please forgive him, Bobbi," he asked, with the sweet affection he had always shown to me. "I promise you, this will not last. It was the Mediterranean sky—the sun, the sea, the stars. It's true, people lose their minds about love there."

I wanted to believe in what he was saying. In spite of the pain, I tried to talk myself into believing that like any other couple, my husband and I were in the middle of a very bad time. At some point, it would change. We would get through it. He would come to his senses, he would want me back. I just had to figure out what it was I needed to do to make that happen. Was it a recipe, some kind of formula?

"Do you love her?" I asked insistently. "What is it about her that's so special?"

This was not a conversation he wanted to have. "It's like talking about apples and oranges," he said evenly. He would not meet my eyes. When his gaze accidentally drifted in my direction, he seemed to look right through me. He was blind to me; I wasn't there anymore.

Charles had to leave his parents' house for all his appointments with various military authorities in Newport and in Washington, in preparation for his work overseas. He would be away about ten days, then back for two days before leaving for Spain. In his absence, I took the boys and went to my mother's—and there, I went nuts.

I called Charles obsessively, three, four times a day, tearfully tracking him up and down the eastern seaboard. I knew I was racing the clock in terms of being able to change his mind—another ten days, and he would be out of the country. "Just tell him his wife called," I said, leaving message after message. "He knows where to reach me."

When I wasn't frantically making phone calls, I was crying. And I stopped eating. Even in my mother's house—even as she baked and cooked and tried to tempt me with the familiar aromas floating from her kitchen, I couldn't bear to smell food, see food, or put it in my mouth.

I stayed in my pajamas all day and let other people take care of my children. When I did get out of bed, it was only to wander from one room to another. My father was gone, which increased my pain ten times over. Dad had liked Charles, I thought. He would know what I should do.

In a couple of days, my mother, sympathetic at first, began to let me know that she was losing patience.

She had always seen me as positive, self-directed, motivated. I had always done whatever I made up my mind to do. That was the house rule: You decided on a goal, you worked hard, and then you got what you worked for. Maybe, Mom suggested, it was time for me to pull myself together, to focus on what we (reminding me I had two children) needed to do next. There was the small matter of a place to live. A job. A life.

"And besides, I always thought Charles was a dud anyway," she said one morning at the breakfast table.

I nearly choked on my English muffin. "What? You

thought he was a *what*?" I was so astonished I almost caught myself smiling.

"A dud," she said calmly. "He was never as full of life as you were. Your father liked him well enough, I guess, but I . . . well, I never really understood what you saw in him."

"Are you saying I should just give up?" I asked. "That I should quit on this marriage?"

"I'm not going to tell you what to do," she said. "But staying in bed, feeling sorry for yourself, not eating, not taking care of your own children—isn't that a kind of quitting?"

As usual, her common sense cut through the drama—I agreed, it was high time to take off the flannel pajamas and get out of the house. We decided to head into town for an afternoon of shopping. I hadn't bought any clothes for a long time; besides, I'd lost so much weight, nothing fit anymore.

As we walked through the familiar front doors of Goldberg's Department Store in Rome, Mom tried to manage the two boys as I grabbed an armload of clothes (and a black lace nightgown) and disappeared into the dressing room. At one point, Nick came barreling into the dressing room with an important announcement. "Mommy, Lexi climbed up in the store window, and he just knocked one of those model ladies down!" He took one horrified look at me and ran right back out onto the floor. "Mommy's in there with a silly black thing on!" he yelled.

One son was tipping mannequins over in a display window, the other was describing his mother's lingerie to the world, and my mother had clearly been out-matched. I could hear someone outside the dressing room anxiously looking for the person responsible for the wild little boys. Only a few weeks before, I had been a happy violin teacher, the contented wife of a navy officer, and mother of two well-behaved children. What the hell had happened to my life?

A day or two later, I ran into an old high-school friend who lived right across the street. Everyone was making plans for our high-school reunion, she said—was I going to come? And there was some news. "Brian lives in New York City now," she said. "He just got divorced, and he has custody of his little boy—can you imagine? You know, if you're going to be around awhile, maybe you should look him up."

I packed up the boys and went back to New Jersey, hoping one last hope: to somehow change Charles's mind in the few days remaining before he left for Europe. Thinking of the black nightgown in my suitcase, I swore I would never take anything or anyone for granted again. I would be the *best* wife, the *best* mother, the *best* whatever it took.

Within minutes of arriving at the house, however, I knew I didn't stand a chance. Nothing had changed—not the look on his face, not the tone of his voice, not the obvious fact that even when he was standing right in front of me, my husband's mind and heart were someplace else.

More than a little desperate, I left the house and went for a walk. When I found a pay phone, I reached for the piece of paper in my pocket and called Brian in New York.

He seemed both pleased and surprised to hear from me; it had been ten years since we had seen each other, and there was a lot of ground to cover. We knew we'd probably bump into each other at the reunion—but wouldn't it be fun to get together before that? We made arrangements to meet a few days later, in a park near Fort Lee; I would bring my boys and we would spend the afternoon catching up.

After I hung up, I went right back to the house and told Charles about the phone call and the upcoming meeting with my old—and divorced—friend. But it didn't faze him at all.

As shattered as I was, I was surprised to find myself worried about him. For someone who had always operated cautiously and deliberately, who always took time to make decisions and rarely took risks, Charles seemed to me to be in an odd kind of danger now. His wife, his children, his marriage—he was walking away from it all. Even more astonishing was this: Music was like religion for me, it meant that much. For Charles, that equivalent was the navy. Yet he was perfectly prepared to throw it all away. For the first time in his life, he had allowed himself to be ruled completely by his emotions.

The morning he left for Spain, I drove him to the

airport. There, he kissed the boys good-bye, picked up his bags, and turned away, walking purposefully to the departure gate. Our marriage had come unraveled almost as fast as it had begun ten years before, and I knew, as the kids clung to my legs and cried, that there was not one damn thing anyone would ever be able to do about it.

Beginning Again

There are probably as many reasons for a marriage to end as there are reasons to try and keep it together, but it's so hard to have any perspective when you're standing in the middle of the wreckage. The saddest thing, of course, is that most human beings have to learn their lessons the hard way. Why does it almost always take a heartbreak, a loss—of something, of someone—to make us pay better attention? Just because I didn't see any signals doesn't mean Charles hadn't been sending them, maybe for years. Hindsight, of course, is always twenty-twenty.

At any rate, the woman who took her two little boys and went off to meet her old friend Brian in a leafy green park was not the person he had known in school. Far from being the spunky, energetic, confident girl he remembered, I felt lightheaded, frail, and more than a little confused, as though I was stumbling out of a bad bout of flu. *Maybe this is a mistake, I thought. Maybe this is the last thing I should be doing today.*

When I saw him, though, all my second thoughts evaporated. This wasn't some scary blind date, it was a visit with a dear, old friend. A handsome old friend, who looked much as he always had—ruddy and freckled, his smile open and welcoming. Dressed casually in sneakers, jeans, and a worn flannel shirt, Brian was about as far removed from Charles and his uniform as any man could possibly be, and he was immediately warm and affectionate to Nick and Alexi.

At first, our conversation was cautious and tentative, but within minutes it felt like all the years that we had been out of touch had never happened. We spoke, of course, about our collapsed marriages. While I was still in some sort of limbo about mine, his was definitely over, and he had custody of his young son, Timmy, who was almost five years older than Nick.

Although Brian had indeed gone to New York to attend Union Theological Seminary after graduating from Amherst, he did not, after all, become a minister. Instead, he was a writer—in fact, he had written a book of interviews with people on death row (he was adamantly against the death penalty), and it would be published quite soon.

His liberal beliefs and progressive opinions had only

become stronger during the years that social activism
and protest had risen across the country. He wasn't just
living in New York City, he was living up in East Harlem, on Lexington Avenue, and his son was going to an
alternative public elementary school in the same neighborhood.

As Brian talked about politics, about the kind of
reporting and research that had gone into writing his
book (at one point he and several others had chained
themselves to a fence in Florida to protest an execution,
and went to jail for it), I envied his sure-footedness and
his conviction. *I don't even know what I think about
things, let alone what I'm going to do next*, I thought.

Usually, women whose husbands leave them for another woman are left, literally, holding the fort: a house,
a home, perhaps a job—at the very least, a familiar
place to get one's bearings. I had none of that. Even
worse, I had no credit rating of my own, no experience
paying the bills or dealing with the financial manage-
ment of a household. Those decisions had always been
made by Charles.

I had spent the previous ten years in some kind of
political and social time warp, much of it outside the
country. Even when history was being made right in
front of me, I didn't recognize it. "In 1971, when I was
a student at B.U.," I told Brian, "I saw police and the
National Guard moving through the Boston streets and
thought it was a parade. But they were gearing up for
the demonstrations after the Kent State shootings!"

I had never even voted in a national election, I told

him. I always handed the absentee ballot to Charles and he did it for me. I didn't know for sure who he had voted for each time, although I always assumed it was a Republican.

Brian just shook his head at this. "I can't believe this is who you grew up to be," he said, only partly joking.

Halfway through our meeting in the park, it became quite apparent to both of us that we were flirting with each other, and that the old attraction was still there. And we certainly weren't in high school anymore. It was with great anticipation, then, and a couple of half-embarrassed grins, that we arranged to meet again for our upcoming high-school reunion.

And there, at that reunion, the dark and heavy cloud that had enveloped me in Greece, followed me to New Jersey, and even invaded my mother's house, began to lift. On Friday night, we got together with old friends in a local bar, drinking beer and laughing about the memories as somebody kept feeding quarters into the jukebox. I wore jeans—when was the last time I'd worn jeans?

The next night, I got all dressed up for the dinner and dance, asking Mom's opinion and checking the mirror at least five times before I allowed myself to leave the house. I wasn't a spurned wife or a frazzled mother, I wasn't a homeless, possessionless reject—I was the object of someone's romantic attention. It was exciting and fun, and at the same time very comfortable, almost familiar. After all, I had known this man for most of my life.

After that weekend, Brian went back to the city, I went back to my mother's, and every day or so we had marathon long-distance phone calls. "You should just bring the boys and come to New York," he said. "I've got these friends who have a great apartment. They're going to Maine for the summer. Maybe you could sublet their place while they're away, and try to figure out everything from here."

I was intrigued by the idea. My mother was skeptical at first, but admittedly relieved. After all, the zombie daughter was finally up and around, changing clothes on a regular basis, wearing a little makeup, taking some interest in Nick and Alexi, and talking about plans for the future. "You're smiling again," Mom said. "I guess that's something."

Before I left for New York, I went to the cemetery to visit my father's grave. As I stepped out of the car, and the boys ran ahead of me, I was suddenly aware that I had my diaphragm in my purse. *He'll know*, I thought. In that moment, I absolutely believed that Dad would look right through the purse and know what I was planning to do—have premeditated sex, with a man who was not my husband! Quickly, I went back to the car, opened the trunk, and stashed the purse inside. I don't know what I thought I had accomplished once I slammed down the trunk lid, but in any case, I felt a little better standing next to my father's grave.

Mom had had the Kahlil Gibran quote carved at the top of Dad's tombstone. *Love knows not its depth until the hour of separation.* "Everything is different now," I whispered to him. "Everything has changed, and I have to change, too."

We arrived at Grand Central Station in the middle of a steamy July day in 1980. Brian met us, with a big smile on his face and holding a single long-stemmed rose. As we stumbled out into the hot sun (it was 100 degrees), I felt like I'd been catapulted not only into a new life, but onto an entirely different planet. New York City may seem an unlikely place for reflection, but it was here that I began the process of unweaving, and reweaving, the tapestry of my life.

Our sublet was a just-right-for-us apartment up on Park Avenue and 96th Street. My landlords had two little boys of their own, and when the family went to Maine for the summer, most of their toys had stayed behind in New York. Since our belongings were still in California, it was a relief to be able to move into a place that needed nothing in order for us to be safe and comfortable. Nick and Alexi settled in reasonably well, although I hadn't yet been entirely truthful with Nick about where his dad was and when, if ever, he would be back. To tell them the truth would have meant telling it to myself first, and I wasn't all the way there yet.

Brian and I spent most of every day together. Sometimes we had my two boys (Brian's son was with his mom that summer), the other times we had the luxury of baby-sitters and time alone. We walked for hours, heading in no particular direction. We went to movies and free concerts in Central Park, we window-shopped, we ate ice cream and Italian ices from street vendors. Even now, I can remember the exhilaration and freedom of coming up out of the subway station near Times Square late one hot summer night, just another anonymous couple in the middle of hundreds of others, all of us surrounded by the heat and the light and the noise of the city. When he took me in his arms and kissed me, right there in front of everybody, I knew I was a very long way from the life I'd been living just a few months before.

Although he continued to live in his own apartment, Brian spent most nights with me. A confirmed vegetarian, he nevertheless enjoyed messing up a kitchen as much as I did, although he had a dismaying dependence on eggs. The man could make a mean soufflé, and teased me unmercifully about the "easy-cheat" omelet pan I used. In turn, I insulted his reliance on store-bought pie crusts for quiche. It began to be a silly competition between us, one I could easily win with homemade ravioli, vegetable lasagne, Greek *spanikopita*, and apple pie with my mother's crust recipe.

He often told me that I was interesting-looking— not beautiful in the cool WASP style which was very much the national ideal in the years we were both growing up, but in a way that was specifically Mediterranean—Italian, emotional, fiery, everything done with great drama. His earliest impressions of me were formed when he watched me playing violin in the orchestra, he said—passionate, almost theatrical. For a woman whose trusted husband had just dealt the ultimate rejection, those words were powerfully seductive.

He did, however, have a big problem with the juice-can hair rollers I'd worn to bed almost every night since I was a teenager, to tame my wild Italian curls. At one point in college, I even had my brother iron my hair! "Oh, no, you don't," said Brian, laughing, the first night he saw me wearing the headgear. "Those are gone!"

To my great joy, Brian was terrific with the kids. He always played with Timmy, roughhousing with him and teasing him affectionately, and he easily extended that attitude to Nick and Lexi. God knows they needed it. He tried to be even-handed with all three boys, but Nick presented a challenge; simply put, he was becoming difficult. Until that summer, he had been the adored oldest son—now, his dad had disappeared, Tim was the big brother, Lexi was the darling baby, and Nick was the truculent middle child.

To his everlasting credit, Brian was willing to be whatever Nick needed—an older friend, a strong hand on the shoulder, a calming influence. And unlike me, Brian really was calm. Over and over at night, Nick would get out of bed—he'd come down the stairs ten times, and Brian never lost his temper. "Okay, Nick, go back upstairs now, it's time for bed." In the meantime,

I was exploding. "Get out of here, I've had enough of this!" A wailing, flailing, screaming Italian mother. There was a lot being written about the need for men to be gentle, and that certainly applied to the way Brian dealt with the kids. He had just gotten custody of his son, and he was determined he was going to do the job right.

As it began to look more and more like I would be staying in the city with Brian after the summer was over, we decided that no matter how much I dreaded it, I had to fly out to California and retrieve what was mine from the boxes in the house at Port Hueneme. I knew that Charles was in Spain and the house was empty; nevertheless, by the time I arrived, my stomach was churning with anxiety.

It was a beautiful house, light and airy and spacious, close to the Pacific Ocean. Had things been different, Charles and I and the boys would have made our home under its roof. And so, within a few minutes of being inside it, I just fell apart—overwhelmed by being surrounded by our possessions, our furniture, the objects we had collected in our travels. Wedding pictures, wine glasses, pottery and dishes that I'd made. Snapshots of the boys on the beach at Nea Makri. The crate of violins we bought with such optimism. Our history.

In the short time that Brian and I had been involved, I had gone from being totally devastated to feeling somewhat optimistic, even happy. In many ways, I was more alive and vital than I'd felt in years; in fact, I was as emotionally and physically fulfilled as I had ever been. As I became aware of the changes inside me, I was also coming to a small but growing understanding of the affair that cost me my husband.

It's a cliché, of course, but as time goes by, even the most solid married couples sometimes forget to take care of—to nurture—the physical side of their relationship. This is especially true once the babies start coming. Almost without anyone noticing, the sensual connection between a man and a woman—the very thing that made them lovers in the first place—takes second or even third place to the needs of a child, the demands of careers, and the responsibilities of daily life. There's so much else to manage, to do—and God knows I had always been driven to *do*, to accomplish the task, to cross it off the day's list. Now Brian was telling me to slow down, to listen, to touch and be touched, to focus on what had awakened between us. It was this, I knew, that Charles and I had never shared—and so he had found it with someone else.

There I was, sitting on the floor in what could have been our home, three thousand miles from my children and the lover who was making me happy, surrounded by the evidence of a marriage I wasn't quite ready to consign to the trash heap. After all, it was a way of life I had been brought up to believe in. "Maybe now that we've both learned a few lessons," I thought, "we could put the marriage back together."

And so, like the gambler who just can't seem to walk away from the table even when his pockets are empty, I placed a call to Charles in Spain, and told him where

I was and what I was feeling. "I understand now what happened to you," I said, "because it's happened to me, too." Maybe this separation had made us wiser. For the sake of the boys, and for all we had once promised and shared, couldn't we take what we learned and make things right? "Let me make a home here," I asked, "and we can be a family again."

The answer, of course, was the same as it had been since the night I'd discovered them embracing in the moonlight. He was still in love with her. Our marriage was over, I simply had to get it through my head: That door was closed and he would never open it again. "Take what you want from the house, Bobbi," he said, "and go back to New York."

To his credit, Brian's response (for of course I called him afterward) was even-handed and pragmatic. "What did you expect?" he asked quietly. "That's who he is. It's time you found out who *you* are. Why don't you come home and get to work on that?"

My aunt Mary, my mother's sister, was living in California at the time. She agreed to come to Port Hueneme and help me sort through my things. "You know, Bert," she said as we worked, "all this grieving for him, it's not worth it. The marriage is over, and it's high time for you to understand that—really understand it—and move on."

Charles and I put a price on everything we had. We agreed on the numbers and then divided everything up; if I wanted the items themselves, fine, otherwise he paid me the agreed-upon value of it. I ended up with some furniture, some tapestries, some pottery, the wheel and kiln, $14,000—and, of course, the violins.

At the end of the summer, Brian and I found an apartment in which we could all live together—a two-story loft on East 124th Street in a borderline but affordable section of East Harlem. There was more than enough room for all three boys, plus space for Brian to do his writing and have a darkroom; for me, at last, there was a sense that I could unpack and settle in someplace. Of course, just across the street from us was an abandoned building frequented by drug dealers. My kids could look across the street almost any time of the day or night and clearly see behavior that would have mortified their grandparents. As we carefully explained to them why some people lived differently than we did, often struggling with terrible circumstances, I sometimes felt like I was walking through a new minefield, watching closely as my sons got their first serious, sometimes painful, education in the disparity between the way life should be and the way it often is.

For parents, the greatest risk when the real world begins to reveal itself is the possibility that the hard information won't translate in the way we hope, and that our children will become fascinated by—even caught up in—behavior whose very danger makes it alluringly seductive. As naïve as I may still have been about many things that summer, I wasn't naïve about the city and its potential to wreak havoc on my children.

Yes, it was a new life for all of us, with many creative challenges, but it could spin out of control just as quickly as a car on a rain-slick road. The only weapons I had were my determination to be vigilant and my faith that my voice (which was growing louder by the day) would be the one Nick and Lexi would always be able to hear above all the other voices shouting for their attention.

Putting Down Roots

The Manhattan neighborhood known as Harlem takes up eight square miles, bounded on the west by Columbia University and Morningside Heights (where Union Theological Seminary and the Cathedral of St. John the Divine are located); on the east by the East River; on the north by 155th Street; and on the south by the upper reaches of Central Park and 110th Street, also known as Cathedral Parkway. Settled by the Dutch (the city of Haarlem is in Holland), Harlem was New York City's first suburb, connected to the commercial heart of town by the train service which began in the mid1800s.

The Harlem Renaissance that flowered after the

first World War drew some of the most innovative and creative African-American minds in the country to these relatively few city blocks. Real estate speculators, who had overbuilt when the train lines came through, knew a good thing when they saw it, and promptly began the city-honored tradition of gouging rents—which of course forces working people and the poor to pile in on top of one another. Yes, Harlem has been ground zero for every urban blight anyone can imagine, but there is a great history and pride as well, and anyone who dismisses that deserves their own ignorance.

Contrary to myth, much of Harlem is movingly beautiful. There are whole stretches of trees, wide avenues, and elegant Victorians and row houses, many dating from the era when wealthy Manhattanites moved north in the summer to take advantage of the river breezes. It has a venerable church culture, and in the Southern gospel music that came from those churches are the roots of American jazz—Duke Ellington, Charlie Parker, the Cotton Club, the Apollo Theatre.

My neighborhood, East Harlem, also known as *El Barrio* or Spanish Harlem, was heavily Italian through the 1930s (there are grape arbor remnants behind many brownstones, including my own), but there were German and Dutch settlers, too; the bulk of the Latin population has come since World War II. Initially, people came from Puerto Rico, but in later years Spanish-speaking neighbors came from the Caribbean, from South and Central America, and from Mexico.

Music rings from this side of Harlem, too—salsa

king Tito Puente comes from 103rd Street. La Marqueta, the commercial district that stretches east across 116th Street from Park Avenue to Third Avenue, is essentially one little shop after another—tacos, empenadas, watch repair, currency exchange, fresh flowers, bagels, travel agents, and wheeling and dealing for the best prices for jeans and sneakers (which I got quite good at when the boys hit their growth spurts). These days, there's a move on to refurbish the Marqueta and develop the blocks around it; as with much of Harlem, this "empowerment zone" plan depends on political will, a combination of public and private investment, and a commitment at the grassroots level to make it happen.

Even from the first days, I wasn't afraid to be in Harlem. I had been exposed to people of many different cultures and beliefs in Greece, and I saw and dealt with racial tensions in Hawaii. Besides, my introduction to the neighborhood came from Brian, and so initially I viewed it through his eyes. He showed me Harlem's great strength and beauty, both in its history and in its contemporary struggles, as the community coped with the ongoing pressures of immigration, the various financial crises in the city, homelessness, and the ravages of the drug war, which turned into the crack epidemic of the mid-eighties.

An important part of Brian's death-row book was the photographs—portraits, really—that he had taken of each of the inmates he had interviewed. His true interest was photojournalism, and he often walked through East Harlem with a camera around his neck, talking

about the wonderful quality of light—especially the twilight—and being drawn like a magnet to the people he
saw in the streets. "Look at those old guys on that
bench," he'd say, pointing out two Latino men deep in
conversation, their leathery faces giving testimony to
years in the sun.

Most of Brian's friends had gone to Ivy League
schools, and the education they had received was radi-
cally different from mine. In many ways, they occupied
a world I wasn't in. Intellectually and academically, I
often felt self-conscious, even inadequate, in serious
discussions. All those times I had given Charles my absentee ballot to fill out, it was because the outcome
didn't seem to have much to do with me. But now, it
had become apparent that I had no business being a
teacher—and teaching an art form at that—unless I became an informed advocate for the lives of my students
and the world in which we lived.

Central Park East School was founded in 1975 by a
nationally respected visionary in education, Deborah
Meier. When she speaks of the school's history, Debbie
always uses *cofounded* because of her insistence upon
giving credit to the equal participation of teachers, parents, and students. But anyone who has ever had any
experience with CPE will unhesitatingly point to Debbie
as its primary muse and guardian angel. CPE1, the first
elementary school, was followed soon after by CPE2
Elementary, and then River East Elementary. A few

years later, Central Park East Secondary School, seventh through twelfth grade, was added.

CPE's student population is largely Latino and African-American, with a small (but growing) Asian contingent; white enrollment fluctuates from ten to fifteen percent in any given year. When it first opened, its school district, District 4, was described as one of the city's poorest. CPE's mission (as cited in Debbie's 1995 book, *The Power of Their Ideas: Lessons for America from a Small School in Harlem*, published by Beacon Press) was "how to provide at public expense for the least advantaged what the most advantaged bought privately for their own children." In a city where the high-school graduation rate runs a fairly consistent 50 percent, CPE graduates 90 percent of its students; of those, more than 80 percent go on to four-year colleges.

Deborah Meier has a strong handshake, a level gaze, and a direct manner of speaking. I saw immediately that she was unpretentious and unbureaucratic. She was a busy woman, with a million things going on at once, primary among them preparing kids for the real world. Her smile was pleasant, her questions about my teaching experience and goals were to the point, and everything about her said, "Get on with it."

So we did, Nick and I—for that first meeting was less a job interview than it was an audition, as teacher and student. Lifting our violins, we played our version of *Twinkle, Twinkle, Little Star*.

This was hardly Nick's first concert recital; in Greece one Christmas, he had played for an audience of three hundred at our church. When he was three, I taught him the "Twinkle variations." It's a routine I still do with all my beginners—first I play a two-measure intro to let them know which variation to play, then they chime in and I play harmony with them. That Christmas, there stood Nick in front of the congregation, holding a one-tenth-size violin. Together, we played four of the five variations, and as I cued him for the fifth one, he took the violin off his shoulder, put one small hand on his hip, and said with great indignation, "Mommy, you *know* I don't like that variation!" At the time, everybody thought it was charming and funny; now, I realize it was a sign of things to come.

After we played for Debbie, her smile grew even warmer. "Well, Roberta," she said, "if you can interest our kids in learning to play the violin, go for it."

While I had two degrees and was qualified to teach, I was not New York City certified. Debbie couldn't bring me into the elementary school until I had what's called a "common branch" license from the state, which would allow me to teach any grade level in elementary school. In order to get a common branch license, I had to take the National Teacher Exam. There was an English component to it, which I agonized about ahead of time, and then scored in the high-90s percentile. I couldn't help notice Brian's surprise at how well I did.

Not that he regularly put me down, but often there was just the slightest suggestion that he knew more than I did. In the beginning, he was very patient about explaining things—I even think he liked it. But there was so much for me to learn, it must have seemed like my education was taking forever.

That first year, Nick attended CPE kindergarten; Lexi, three, went to a preschool on East 92nd Street, called the Learning Community; the following year, he started a full day in the pre-K class at CPE. By the end of the first year I had forty students; the next year, I expanded to seventy; by the third year, when River East opened, I was teaching violin to kids at all three schools.

The style at CPE, reflecting both the neighborhood and the times, was relaxed and informal—no dress code, no name code: We used first names among colleagues and kids alike; to my students, I've always been Roberta.

I never felt uneasy or uncomfortable at CPE, even from the beginning. It was an elementary school, after all; these were young kids. The education model is based on progressive methods, adapted as needed over the years. The basic idea was open classroom, with each student progressing at his or her own rate. There were many classrooms that contained multi-grade levels. You might see kids at one table working out math problems at a certain level using pattern blocks; across the room, another group solved math problems by measuring how much water in the fish tank would be displaced if they dropped in the pregnant guinea pig.

At first, my violin students were all fifth and sixth graders, but I figured out after that first year that I needed to go younger. Sixth graders graduate; I had to find a way to build a base of kids who kept coming back year after year, getting better each time.

I carried everything around with me—sheet music, violins, bows and cases, my own violin and bow, rosin, extra sponges for chin rests—begging the administrative and custodial staffs in each school for a storage closet for the violins. (Storage space in NYC schools is a perpetual problem, as is classroom space—most of us feel like we're teaching in closets, and quite often, we are.) The worst violin-carrying-day, even now, is at the beginning of the year, when I distribute them to new students or trade up (in size) with the older students, schlepping forty-five or fifty violins from one school building to another. That's why I've always had a hatchback car, so I can fill it up with violins. In addition to being full of violins, the car also contains a glove compartment full of parking tickets—at approximately $200 a month, it's roughly the same cost as putting my car into a parking garage, but more conveniently located to school!

The storage-and-inventory situation suffered a crisis in the mid-1980s. A watershed crisis, I guess you could call it. The violins were stored on the second floor, in a nice closet just off the dance room. During the summer, plumbers who were doing some repair work in the building inadvertently left a cap off one of the pipes that ran above the ceiling over the closet. The pipe sprang a leak, and water poured into the closet. No one knew what had happened until we got back to school in the fall, and I opened the closet to retrieve the violins on distribution day. My heart stopped: The air was dank and moldy-smelling and the instruments were a pile of warped wood, with green mildew growing everywhere. Well, that's the end of the Greek violins, I thought.

The insurance appraiser came almost immediately, and once the reimbursement had been made, we were able to upgrade our violin inventory. It was yet another example to me that a disaster can be turned into something else entirely—if, that is, you don't run screaming from the room in the first five minutes.

I wanted to go further with my own violin study, and possibly even get into performing, but in order to do that I needed a better quality instrument to work with— I was still playing the violin my parents had given me in the tenth grade. I called my cousin Paul LaBella, who lived in Rome, New York, and was a retired violinist from the Utica Symphony. He referred me to a violin shop in Manhattan owned by a family named Tatar. When Pietro Tatar, a talented violin maker, had originally come to the United States from Cremona, Italy, Paul had been his sponsor—he assured me that whatever I found in that shop was likely to be of excellent quality.

When I went to the shop, Pietro had recently died; his son Peter, then in his twenties, was working with his mother to keep the business open and running. After we had talked for a few minutes and I explained what I was looking for, he went to the safe and brought out a beautiful instrument made in 1867 by Andreas Postacchini. The price, he said, was $6,000.

Peter Tatar allowed me to take the violin home for one night, and when I played it, I simply fell in love with it. I appeared early the next morning at Tatar's shop. I had raided the savings account (which contained my divorce settlement) on the way, and handed him $1,500 in cash. I would be back as soon as I could, I promised; in return, he wrote out a receipt that listed a balance due of $4,500. For some reason, after I left, Mr. Tatar started second-guessing himself, and over the weekend he took the violin to a very well-known and respected appraiser, Dario D'Attili. The price I was going to pay, D'Attili informed him, was far, far less than the Postacchini was worth.

When I returned with the balance, I was told he couldn't sell the violin to me for that price. Ever my mother's daughter, I dug in my heels and stuck to the bargain: There was no way I was going home without this violin, no way I would accept his change of heart, and no way I could pay more for it. I strongly insisted that he honor the numbers clearly written there on his own receipt. His face took on a resigned expression— he was getting married that weekend. I went home with the violin, whose worth and meaning has appreciated many times over in the years since.

At around the same time, I became involved with a small chamber orchestra that met regularly in Greenwich Village; many of its members also went each summer to a chamber music conference in Bennington, Vermont. Some of these friends recommended that I study with a teacher named Joyce Robins. Retired now, she had a reputation as a real troubleshooter; for the most part, she taught only professional artists, and was known as something of a doctor, because she had a unique gift for diagnosing what was wrong with any individual technique and showing you how to overcome it in a few lessons.

At the same time that she was helping me work within my limitations, she recognized and praised my sound and musicality. What she did was therapeutic, almost healing. What I learned from her not only helped me, but it helped me learn how to teach.

Every time Joyce Robins would teach me something—or help me relearn something—I discovered a new way to teach the kids.

I took all the "new" ideas and turned them into childlike images—tickle tunnel, walking fingers, stop signs—any image that would make it easier for the kids to grasp what I was saying. The language I use when explaining things to little kids is simple—one-word, two-word images. Shortcuts. It's like training a puppy— each word must always have a precise meaning. I send signals, I overexaggerate, and the terminology has to be consistently true all the time, each time, for every kid, because I don't have the time or liberty to customize it for each of them—I'm teaching everybody at once.

The good news is, the beginners believe everything I tell them. Most of them are too little to know to be afraid of the challenge of learning to play an instrument, to be daunted by it. They have a little kid's concept of time; they don't start out thinking, "I'll never get this." The bad news is, of course, they're babies. They get tired and hungry, they get fidgety, they have to be taken to the bathroom. And beginners always have to tie their shoes before they start to play. Maybe it's a delaying tactic, maybe its their first command from home, the first one they really lock into. I say, "Let's begin," they look down at their feet, see that their shoelaces are untied and—uh-oh—*Tie your shoes, tie your shoes*. I could save countless minutes every year by insisting that beginners wear Velcro'd sneakers!

For the little ones, learning to play an instrument is a way to teach them to focus their thinking, to screen out what's not important. There's so much information they have to take in: for instance, where everything goes—fingers, thumb, pinky, elbow, shoulders, back, feet, chin, nose, belly. And then there's the violin itself, and the bow. Standing still is the hardest thing; these are wiggly little kids, and they have to learn to be still. They have to really concentrate on that.

I really believe that if you give children too many choices before they're formed in their habits and their thinking, they'll always either fumble the choice or take advantage of the offer. When you say, "What do you want for breakfast?" it'll be one extreme or the other: ice cream, or a complete inability to decide. Plus it takes too much time—hours later, you're still there, tying shoes and making choices. But if you say, "You may have cereal or French toast, two choices, pick one," you create a different scenario, with a little bit of control and a manageable amount of choice. I'm never going to go into class and say, "Well, what would you like to play today?" Well, actually, maybe I might—for the fifth and sixth graders, at the end of a really good session.

By the mid-eighties, there were more than 120 kids in the violin program, ranging from beginners all the way through sixth graders, and including Nick and Lexi. For our three-school end-of-the-year concert, I start rounding everybody up in April, even the older kids who have graduated from the elementary schools. I always like to have at least one piece that is not abridged, is much more challenging, and offers an opportunity for the more advanced students and the graduates to play at a higher level. For weeks in advance, we have two-hour rehearsals at my house, on weekends and evenings after school. Often there are more than thirty kids at the house, their violin cases strewn from one end of the living room to the other, their music stands in the kitchen. Afterward, we always have pizza.

As the kids come back year after year, we've all become more involved in each others' lives. I know their parents; they all know my family; we work hard together. And the relationships with these families are the ones that sustain me, good times and bad.

Home

I was such a dependent person when my relationship
with Brian began that I must have decided, somewhere deep inside my head and heart, that Brian would
now play Charles's role, and we would simply live happily forever. Without being consciously aware of it, I
had exchanged one man for the other. Once I was divorced and a little time had passed, I hoped that we
would be married.

Brian, however, increasingly found ways to let me
know that he didn't believe he was a candidate for marriage, at least not then. Nothing was forever, he said;
besides, "People die." He was traveling a lot for work—
there were freelance assignments, and another book in

the works—and he was gone for weeks at a time. He was more and more attracted to women who were real intellectuals—often writers—and he often let me know when he'd met someone interesting. And I was too strict with the boys, too shrill, too negative, he said—didn't I know that kind of parenting could really harm a child?

As much as I was finding my way at school, I felt like I was losing my way at home. I was just a little off balance all the time. When Brian was out of town I wondered what he was doing, who he was with. When he was home he liked to listen to loud rock and roll while he worked, and although I tried to get into it, it gave me a headache. So he got a pair of headphones and wore them constantly, which only made me feel more isolated. I couldn't help but replay scenes from the end of my marriage. I had missed the signs then; perhaps I should be watching more closely this time. But if I looked too closely, I might end up creating problems where none existed. I told myself I was being paranoid. Stupid. This wasn't Charles, it was Brian, my soul mate. We were the people who had made a promise to always be honest with each other.

I took Nick and Lexi to North Carolina for a mini family reunion; my brother lived there, and my sister, who had just had a baby, joined us. When I returned three weeks later, it was clear that something had happened while I was away. The air was heavier, and it wasn't just the humidity. It soon became clear that he had been unfaithful. "I never made any promises," he said, and I had to admit he was right—he never had.

We decided to try to stay together, and we did, for about a year and a half after that—three years, all told. But we never got back what we'd once had. I had always believed in monogamy, in commitment, and that was still what I wanted. I may have been wiser than I was when I married Charles, and the juice-can rollers may have been long gone, but basically I was the same woman inside. Something in our relationship had been broken, and no matter how much I wanted it to be otherwise, it couldn't be repaired.

Although I wasn't completely sure what the future of my relationship would be, I did know that East Harlem was now my home; I also knew that I was not, at heart, an apartment person. Whether Brian came along or not, I wanted a place of my own. I wanted some sense of permanency, of possession. In fact, I yearned for it.

Through the grapevine I heard about an elderly couple on 118th Street who were interested in selling their house, ideally to an Italian family with children. The house, a narrow brownstone with four floors, was in what had been a venerable Italian neighborhood. At one time it had been big-time Mafia; just up the street was Patsy's Pizzeria, reportedly Frank Sinatra's all-time favorite—he supposedly had Patsy's pizzas flown to him all over the country. A few blocks away, on the corner just across from River East School, was Rao's, a tiny

Italian restaurant whose marinara sauce is legendary and where the stretch limos line up in the evenings long before the doors open.

The house itself was very dark and claustrophobic inside—dark walls, dark artificial wood paneling, small rooms upstairs and down, a living room painted a garish shade of orange, a wide hall (which seemed a strange way to use space, given the tiny rooms), and an odd little sanctuary off the kitchen that contained a statue of the Madonna and a big, glowing fish tank. However, I knew from the first minute I stepped inside, what it would all look like once it was gutted, with the walls knocked down and the main floor opened up to the light and space I just knew was under all that darkness.

For three months, I courted the old Italian couple, trying to persuade them that we were the perfect family for their house. Every day after school, I brought Italian cookies and big blocks of cheese, and we sat and talked— about the house, about the history of our families, about whatever I could think of that might persuade them that we were the very family they'd been looking for. Finally they gave in. Debbie Meier vouched for my job security so that I could get a mortgage, and also signed a guarantee letter so I could get my very first charge card. I was exuberant for about twenty minutes—and then the 118th Street Construction Follies began.

For months, the house was like a bombed-out shell, with construction chaos in the center. I couldn't afford to hire a general contractor, so I was it. The boys and I would drive over after school to check on progress, and the wave of sound coming from inside the house would hit the car like a brick. One guy had salsa blaring on his cassette player; another guy had hip-hop; a third guy favored heavy metal rock. The resulting cacophony was a big, noisy metaphor for what was going on in-side—no one was communicating with anybody else, and none of them had much use for me. Nick walked around in a kind of despair, his little-boy shoulders hunched up under his ears. "Mom, why are you doing this?" he'd ask. "Why isn't Brian here helping us?"

Actually, Brian was there quite often, especially in the beginning. We had a huge Dumpster out front, and he'd come over and work with me on the weekends, tearing out the old walls and hauling the plaster to the Dumpster. But the tension between us was running high. He was convinced I'd been robbed when I bought the house, criticized almost every decision I made about the reconstruction, and said my own stubbornness was setting me up for more rip-offs to come. By the time the boys and I actually moved into the house, it was without Brian.

He was right about the rip-offs, however, and it took me a while before I could spot them. For instance, there was Ernie, the Sheetrock guy, and his partner Al, the electrician. I gave them $5,000 in advance, to buy everything they needed, but for days on end, nothing showed up. "Where's the Sheetrock?" I asked. "Where are the light switches?" Finally one day, a dump truck pulled up in front of the house, and Al and Ernie started to unload it.

"Wait a minute," I said. "Why does all this Sheet-rock have wallpaper on it?"

"Oh, that's the new thing they do now, to protect the Sheetrock and add extra insulation to the walls," they told me, looking disturbingly like my violin kids who swore they'd practiced the night before when it was so obvious they hadn't.

"But it's all different kinds of wallpaper," I said. "Flowers and stripes. Are you sure this is insulation? I don't think so." My trusty subcontractors were pulling Sheetrock out of abandoned buildings. I had spent $5,000, and not one cent went for new Sheetrock.

Nor electrical expertise. I discovered that Al's cosmetically perfect fixtures were fake; literally, there was nothing behind them. That was the end of Al.

But for some reason, I felt sorry for Ernie. He hadn't been out of jail very long (so of course he pleaded with me not to call the cops about the Sheetrock) and I had met his wife and two little kids. I really believed he was trying to get it together. He swore he would stay and work his hardest, to make up for the money they'd taken, so I decided, "OK, I'll let you strip the banister." *And if that works,* I thought, *then he can strip all the molding on the parlor floor—all the woodwork in the house, as a matter of fact.* But Ernie, I discovered, was a serious alcoholic, and every day, he was bottoming out in my stairwell. The banister took weeks, and finally, that was the end of Ernie, too.

Different tools "disappeared" from the site every night—one guy's hammer, another guy's saw, somebody's extension cord, a few boxes of nails. Wanting to keep peace on the project (and not wanting to accuse anyone in particular, although they all stood ready to accuse each other), I naively kept replacing what was lost until one day I hit my limit in both budget and tolerance. "That's it, guys," I announced. "I'm done. From now on, you're each responsible for your own tools." Miraculously, nothing ever disappeared from the site again.

And there were a few other problems. For instance, where my garden is now—the roses, the clematis— there was no garden. I was so blinded by possibility when I looked out the back door, I thought, "Oh, good, there's a wonderful yard for the kids!" After we moved in, I bought a big round white table and beautiful chairs to go with it. Little did I know how futile that was. The building next door, I discovered, was a tenement build- ing, complete with transient squatters and drug dealers. And they couldn't be bothered to take their garbage down to the cans in the front of their building, so they just pitched it out their windows—right into my new backyard.

And what, I wondered, were all those bright tiny objects scattered all over the yard like confetti? Red, green, yellow, blue—the plastic caps from crack vials. And discarded needles. Every few weeks, I hired guys who put on big boots and big gloves and went out into the yard like they were taking on a battlefield. With industrial-size garbage bags, they swept the yard clean. A month or so later, it would all have to be done again.

I was told that in order to get the garbage pitching to stop, I had to file a police report each time I saw it happening, which I determinedly did. Ultimately, it took ten years of gritting my teeth and fighting back. The building next door was sold to a new owner, and gradually, the old tenants disappeared. Now there's a very nice super there—I let him know whenever there's a problem, which isn't very often. But it was a very long time before I could actually sit out in the garden with a glass of my own wine without fearing I'd be whacked in the head by someone else's bottle.

The fireplace, which I had thought was only boarded up, had never been a working fireplace at all; it was a facade. *All right,* I thought, *at least I can make it look real, with a mantel and decorative brickwork.* But the bricklayer (who was not—surprise, surprise—a professional) kept cementing the bricks wrong; off-kilter, not plumb, looking like he'd thrown them, one at a time, from across the room onto the wall. Three times I asked him to redo it, carefully sketching the way I wanted it to look. Three times, he took it apart and put it back together badly. Finally, I did it myself. Harry (the new electrician) helped me mix the mortar.

The plumber, Marty, turned out to be a prince, and he's still my plumber to this day. Unlike the others, he didn't insist on the money up front, but let me make payments, $300 every two weeks, long after the project was done—I finally finished paying him four years later. Not only did he solve the Sheetrock problem, he found someone reliable—Gabe—to install it. Ultimately, Gabe did all the plastering, too, and I paid him the same way I paid Marty—cash every two weeks, for a very long time.

After the Al-and-Ernie Sheetrock mess, I bought all the material myself; to save money, I picked everything up from the hardware store rather than pay for delivery. After school every day, Gabe would give me a list of what to buy the next day. I'd place the order in the morning on my way to school and pick it up on my way home. I probably lugged one hundred cans of joint compound into the house, and those things are heavy. And I hauled all the carpentry boards, too, and drove to the house with them sticking out through the car windows.

I wandered into a used furniture place up on 123rd Street one day and bought a beautiful old corner cupboard for almost nothing. I didn't have a corner to put it in; however, there was the small matter of the exposed pipes in the corner of the kitchen/dining-room wall. "Hey," I said, "let's cover up those pipes with the cupboard." I sketched out the way I wanted it to go and Gabe built it, cursing every minute of the way. We called it my "Guggenheim boxing."

Now, Harry the new electrician was not licensed—but who could afford a licensed electrician? And he wasn't exactly new, either; he was in his late seventies. But he had a great reputation in the neighborhood, or so I was told. Supposedly, he had wired everybody, and he was quite enthusiastic about wiring us, too. The only problem was, he would forget he was supposed to actually come to the project and *do* it. "Oh, Mom, we've got to go get him," Nick would groan in the morning, and off we would drive to Harry's brownstone. I'd knock on the door and out he'd come, looking sheepish, his white hair sticking out in six directions. "I forgot." On the way back to the house he'd wave at various buildings and say, "See that one? I wired that in 1953. See that one over there? I wired it in 1964."

Harry couldn't see very well, and he stumbled so badly when he walked through the construction debris that Nick would scurry ahead of him, hastily moving woodscraps and wires and tools out of his path. Inevitably, something would get overlooked and then down Harry would crash, apologizing all the way. "Don't worry, don't worry." He'd wave us off. "I'm all right, everything's OK." Or he'd be all the way up near the top of the ladder, with the boys steadying its legs at the bottom, and suddenly he'd say, "Uh-oh. Get me my glasses, somebody!"

"Where are they, Harry?" I'd ask.

Silence. "You know, honey, I can't remember where I left them."

Every day after school, Harry took the three of us to the Delightful Diner on 116th Street for ice cream and coffee, his treat. And he'd tell me what he needed for the next day. They all knew me at the electrical shops in the neighborhood, because I would appear and reappear twice as often as anyone else. I'd order whatever it was that Harry had asked for, but when I gave it to him, he would greet me with a look of complete befuddlement. "No, no, I said breakers, honey," he'd say, shaking his head. "I didn't want a fuse box." And back I'd go to make the exchange.

As the weeks went by, Gabe told me that his work was almost done; it seemed that the time for us to move into the house was approaching. Things would still be rough around the edges, but it would be livable, and whatever remained I could finish on my own. And then came the big surprise.

It was February, Valentine's Day—which I remember very clearly, because over ice cream and coffee at the Delightful Diner, Harry handed me a homemade Valentine greeting, signed "Love, Harry," in crayon. And then he said, "Look, honey, I want to give you this card . . . but I don't know how to tell you this." He paused, then started again. "I never wanted to hurt you, honey— I'm in love with you, really I am." Now he was in tears, shaking his head. "But you know, I just can't seem to remember where all those wires go. I just can't figure it out this time."

"No!" I felt like I'd been dropped on my head.

Sure enough, down in my basement it looked like *Saturday Night Live* was doing a skit about electricians. Multicolored electrical wire, resembling nothing so much as exploded pasta, seemed to have burst from the wall. Evidently we'd hired Harry too near the end of his electrical career.

It didn't help when an inspector from Con Edison showed up. At this point we had a few working lights, but unbeknownst to me, we didn't have any permits, and we had never arranged for—or paid for—a legitimate hookup. We were stealing kilowatts. I was called out of River East School to come home immediately; it was an emergency.

When I got home, Marty the plumber was there trying to negotiate. The Con Ed inspector suggested that maybe we could work a deal: He'd keep my wires a secret in exchange for $450. The alternative: I could be fined a much greater amount or possibly even be put in jail. He gave me a couple of days to think it over and pay up.

I'd had enough. I was out of money, out of patience, and besides, this was extortion, plain and simple. I went immediately to Con Ed and told them exactly what had happened. They dealt with him, and settled with me for a little under $200 for the permits and the power already used. Then they let me go home. Home.

Son Rise

When Nick was about nine, Deborah Meier called me into her office for what she called a very serious matter; for weeks, she said, his teachers had been coming to her with complaints. He was constantly in trouble for fighting—in the classroom, on the playground, it didn't matter where he was. "You have to do something about this, Roberta," Debbie said with what I knew were equal parts compassion and determination. "He's lost control, and I think it means that you have, too. For the sake of everyone, we cannot let this continue."

She had given him an in-school suspension for two days, which meant he wasn't allowed to go into the classroom, but instead had to sit in the office, which allowed me to continue to do my job. But she insisted that we get family therapy. "Maybe," she said ominously, "Central Park East school isn't for everybody."

At her recommendation, we contacted Ackerman Institute, the family counseling center that often worked with the school. The staff at Ackerman suggested an interesting proposition: If we would allow their therapists-in-training to watch our sessions from the other side of a one-way mirror, the Institute in turn would reduce the fee.

It may be hard to imagine now what a negative and even terrifying connotation the words *therapy* and *family counseling* carried for many people in 1983. If I was somewhat taken aback by the need for it, my family (and Nick's father) were even more upset. Therapy meant mental illness—surely that wasn't the problem here, was it? Wasn't it just a discipline problem? Was I doing something wrong? But in spite of their concerns and objections, I paid little attention. I instinctively knew that this would be the right thing for all of us, especially me.

The house renovation had caused financial upheaval and emotional exhaustion. The relationship with Brian had come to its painful end—he was already involved with someone else. I was frayed around the edges; no wonder my son was, too. Lexi, then seven, watched Nick like a hawk, following him around, imitating his behavior, wanting his approval—it was only a matter of time before he got caught up in the mess as well.

Our first appointment was at 8 P.M., at the end of a long weekday for a tired violin teacher and two little boys. We walked nervously into a nondescript room that was furnished halfway between conference room and living room, with toys scattered on the floor.

The therapist, a pleasant-enough man named Leslie, carefully explained to the boys about the one-way mirror, which fascinated them immediately; in fact, we never walked into that room again that they didn't head right for the mirror and begin making exaggerated gestures, with body language that sometimes verged on the obscene. "We know you're back there, you invisible people," they seemed to be saying with their elbows and their hips and their hand gestures, "and you don't scare us one bit."

In spite of the embarrassing comedy, the therapist brought us down to earth right away. Nick was in trouble, with his explosions of temper and the constant fighting—why, Leslie asked, did he think that was happening?

"But it's not me," Nick said. "It's a bad guy who comes into me, and makes me do bad things. I feel it coming, but I can't make it stop." He didn't have any control over what happened in these instances, he told us. Literally, he felt powerless over what was going on inside and around him.

There were two basic steps to the process we were all engaged in, Leslie explained. First was to devise some kind of workable system for behavioral modification; that is, to actually get Nick to stop the fighting, before he hurt someone or got hurt himself. Second was to search for the reasons, and the solutions, for his behavior.

Together, we came up with what we called a "save"—a secret code or emergency signal that Nick could use that the other kids wouldn't know the meaning of but all the pertinent grown-ups would. It was a two-word signal: first, the name of the nearest grown-up wherever Nick was; second, the word *Nick*. *Debbie, Nick!* That's all he had to say. It meant, "Debbie, it's about to happen, this is Nick, come here fast, help me!"

We drew up a calendar that charted each day, noting the number of fights and saves. At the end of each week, depending on the number of reported no-fight days or saves (which in a way were more valuable, since they indicated conscious attempts at self-control), Nick would be rewarded with a toy called a transformer, a small action figure that was very popular with kids at the time. As each day was crossed off, the irony of the word *transformer* wasn't lost on anyone involved—his teachers, his therapist, his mother. The problem wasn't solved, but slowly, the behavior was changing.

As the weeks passed and the sessions continued, Leslie came to know us all better, and his questions— sometimes only one or two a session—became more acute. And Nick, it appeared, had a few questions of his own. One night, while Lexi collapsed in a sleepy lump over in the toy corner, Nick drew a bead on me. "Why did you make Brian leave, Mommy?" he asked. "And why did you make my daddy go away?"

Grown-ups don't usually go around explaining their private mistakes and sorrows to their kids; however, I thought I had been as open with mine as it was possible to be. Certainly they had seen me in tears, and they had heard the words. Didn't they know that breaking up with Brian was not what I wanted? And if Nick truly believed that I had made Charles leave, then there was something terribly wrong with the way he was translating information.

And there was a third question, one that carried more weight than the others. "Who's going to take care of you, Mommy?" Nick asked.

This was completely devastating. Evidently, this child had come to believe that in the absence of a grown-up man, taking care of me and his little brother had become his job—and he was desperately afraid he wouldn't be able to do it. No wonder he was throwing punches everywhere he turned. He was simply trying to defend himself.

"You have to tell him the truth now, Roberta," Leslie said. "He needs to know what really happened."

As I flashed back on the telephone conversation I'd had with Charles in the empty house in Port Hueneme, the tears started streaming down my face. "Nick, maybe Brian and I aren't going to be together anymore, but he is your friend and Lexi's friend forever. You can call him and see him whenever you want; he said so, and I believe him. As for your dad, I begged him not to leave me. I wanted to stay in the house with you guys and keep our family together. But he just didn't want me anymore. And so he said no."

"He wouldn't even let you try?" Nick sobbed, and at that, the dam broke. The tears rolled down Leslie's face, and from behind the one-way mirror, we could hear the invisible people crying with us.

Nick switched from playing violin to playing the cello at about the same time we were in family therapy. It was as though he was thinking, *How can I hold on to the music but not do what she does?* Not long after that, Lexi also changed instruments, to the piano.

The violin had been a good way for us all to begin together; it introduced the boys to a life of music, to the discipline and the solace that an instrument can bring. But the violin was mine, and the boys had been inundated with it almost since they could walk. Although I had a few twinges of regret, I knew it was time, and right, for them to make these choices.

Nick had always had very good ear with the violin, but he balked when it came to reading music. He had a lazy eye—he had to wear a patch for a while—and reading sheet music felt to him like going back to first grade and starting at "Run, Spot, run" all over again. Exasperated, he started looking at the music once and then memorizing it. When he decided to change instruments, he thought he'd be able to do the same thing with the piano. But you can't get very far on a piano without knowing how to read music, a lot of it at a time, and read it well. So it was the cello for Nick. And I was informed in no uncertain terms that I was *never* to touch that cello.

As for Lexi's decision to switch, when he went to the first couple of concerts that Nick played in with his cello, he heard the little chamber music group that Nick's teacher had put together, and was enthralled by the role the young pianist played in the ensemble. After that, it was the piano for Lexi.

Even when he was little, Nick loved to perform, and he always did it beautifully, starting with the day he sang the Greek liturgy verses in the backseat of the car in Rhode Island. Lexi, who is just as musical as his brother, hates to perform—as a kid, the dread of an upcoming concert built in him for days—weeks—in advance. He got migraine headaches; he got upset stomachs.

When the boys changed instruments, I learned the lesson that all parents must come to, hopefully earlier rather than later: Leave the door open for everything that kids are interested in doing. Yes, you have to juggle and prioritize, but you have to give proper respect to their choices, and find ways to accommodate them if it's possible.

This tidy theory got a little complicated once they both became as active in sports as they were in music, although I was delighted with the activities—I wanted them busy, and I also wanted my violin students to see that boys could be good athletes and musicians at the same time. But I had to make a focused effort to arrange the family schedule around basketball and Little League games, practices, and meetings; plus I went to all their games. Every weekend, we set up the charts together—a double header in Little League on a Wednesday meant adjusting music practice on Tuesday and Thursday. Friday night was Boy Scout night, which they really enjoyed, although it was a deep, dark secret among their friends. I had strict orders that if anybody called while they were at Scouts, I was to say only that Nick and Lexi were "out." And it went without saying that I couldn't tell anyone that Lexi had gotten very adept with the sewing machine, expertly sewing the Scout badges on both their uniforms.

Just as with my family when I was growing up, our own rituals and traditions evolved. Birthday parties were major events—the boys invited as many kids as the house would hold, and I cooked endless pans of *spanikopita*, and lasagne with five-hour sauce. In high school, Lexi once brought the entire Bronx Science varsity basketball team—these were large and hungry boys. Food was key to everything; the kitchen in my house is the main room, both figuratively and literally. The entire ground floor is one open room, just as I'd pictured it before the renovation—the piano sits at the center, with the music stand next to it, and the dog beneath it—and I can stand at the stove while someone else is playing music and see every move they make.

Christmas was a two-edged sword. True to form, I cooked and baked for weeks, all the while rehearsing with my students for the holiday concert at school. I obsessed over the tree in exactly the way my father had, although I was allergic to the resin and the boys had to do all the actual tree wrangling. We would go together after school and pick out the perfect one. Then it would sit in a pail of water in the backyard until we had time to decorate—the water in the pot would freeze, the ice would lock the tree into the pail, and the boys would have to chip away the ice in order to free the tree. Into the house it would come, Nick securing it into the old stand as best he could. Inevitably the tip scraped the ceiling. "Nick, it's lopsided," I'd say.

"It's not," he would answer.

"No, Mom, it's not," Lexi would chime in.

"It is," I would argue.

"Mom, quit it." Nick would order. "That's as good as it gets."

The haggling would continue throughout the decorating process until finally, when it was time for my treasured Nutcracker figure to be placed at the top of the tree, Nick was usually so agitated that he forcibly jammed Nutcracker down on the topmost branch in a less-than-dignified position.

On Christmas Eve we often had company for the annual fresh lobster dinner—the battle was always over who would lift the flailing live lobster up off the floor and into the pot. We also opened our presents on Christmas Eve, in spite of Lexi's great concern about how it was that Santa got to our house the night before Christmas.

For me, the next day spelled only doom: In the

morning, the boys left to spend the rest of their vacation with their father. Sometimes I went to my mother's or my sister's; more often, I found ways to mark time until the door opened and the boys came home.

In the eighth grade, Nick didn't know if he wanted to be a baseball catcher or a cellist. And then I sent him to Greenwood, his first music camp. I talked him into auditioning, and he was accepted with a scholarship. When we were on our way there, while I was driving, he was reading the brochure—all about the farmhouse at the camp's center, and the garden, which all the students were expected to work in. The cook used herbs from the garden, all the meals were organic, with natural ingredients and homemade bread. To me, it sounded like heaven.

To Nick, the closer we got, the more it sounded like some kind of musical organic gardening hell. Yes, he played the cello, but he was also an athlete, a city kid. Gardens? Herbs? He started to protest loudly, and the more he did, the more nervous I became. I looked at the clock on the dashboard—*oh, we're going to be so late,* I thought. I speeded up. "Mom, why did you do this to me?" he kept asking, his voice angrier each time. "Why seven weeks in the woods with organic flour and a bunch of wimps? I mean, it looks like I'm spending the entire summer gardening with nerds!"

I just gripped the steering wheel harder and pushed my foot down on the accelerator. The toll I paid for that day was two speeding tickets. By the time I dropped him off, he was furious and forlorn. I left feeling like I'd abandoned my kid to some awful fate, which he would hate, and then hate me—all the usual second-guessing that a parent does.

A few days later, I got a jubilant phone call. "Mom, this is the most wonderful place I've been in my life!" He was surrounded by other musicians, which certainly wasn't the case at his school. And some kids could even beat him in Ping-Pong! He had been playing in a string quartet and had discovered what I had discovered so many years before—that sharing this very emotional activity with other people was a joyful, powerful experience. "I don't want it to end," he said. "I don't want it to end."

As much as I knew I was right to buy our house, there's no question we arrived at a rough time for this city and for this neighborhood. There was gunfire someplace within earshot almost every night—maybe it was blocks and blocks away, but the sound carried nevertheless, and it often felt like we were living on the frontier. We had to learn to be streetwise—to pay attention to what time it was, which block we were on, what message our body language was sending.

The house was robbed one night when we were away. There were a few nights when I had to yank my violin students away from the front window. One evening at dinner, we heard what we thought were firecrackers or a car backfiring, and discovered the next day that it had been a drive-by that left two young men dead. Another night, when Lexi was in the fourth grade, he sat at the dinner table and casually stopped my heart by saying, "When I was walking to school the other day, I had to cross the street because I didn't want to get caught in the crossfire."

I resolved that I had to know where my boys were all the time, and when they were late (which Lexi always was, and never called to let me know), I simply went nuts.

The worst time of year in my neighborhood was the Fourth of July—or rather, the week before, during, and after, because the display went on in the streets for days at a time. It had less to do with patriotism than it did with a show of power, primarily among the drug dealers, who were the only ones around with money to burn— literally. They spent thousands of dollars on my street alone. Forget sparklers, pinwheels, Roman Candles, M-80s; night after night, the spectacle outside the house rivaled what was going on in Beirut at the same time. One year, the roof of my car had a big gouge in it from an explosive device they called a "tin can" that was thrown from the building next door in the middle of the night. I tried to imagine the result if it had landed on a person instead of a car roof. The day after the Fourth, acrid smoke still hung in the air, and not one piece of sidewalk or street was visible, all of it covered in bright red firecracker paper.

One July afternoon, a group of my chamber music friends was sitting in my living room preparing to play string quartets. One of them, Steve McGhee, was and is a fine violin maker and expert repair guy, with his own violin shop at 104th and West End. Steve had made his own cello and it was beautiful. That afternoon, when he took off the instrument's soft cover, the violist said, "Steve, what on earth happened to your cello?"

He looked down at the instrument in some alarm; sure enough, it looked as though someone had punched a hole near one of the f-holes. Steve shook the cello to see if the soundpost was still standing, and was rewarded with the sound of a rattle inside. A piece of shriveled-up metal fell out.

"I think that's a bullet," someone said. I immediately grabbed it and went out to the sidewalk, stopping the first person I saw, who happened to be one of the guys from the tenement next door. "Do you know what this is?" I asked.

He held it up, examined it, then nodded. "Bullet from a twenty-two Magnum," he said.

The night before, Steve had dropped his cello off at my house in preparation for the following day's session, and then he'd driven home. The cello had been left behind my couch, right by the front window. Had a bullet come through that window? We checked—no bullet hole, no broken glass. I suddenly had an absurd picture of someone having snuck into my house via the fire escape, silently coming down the stairs, and blowing a hole in the cello during the night—but of course that made no sense. Who was the culprit, we wondered?

Then Steve and I remembered—while he was taking the cello out of his car trunk the night before, there had been a sudden volley of firecrackers. Hardened Fourth of July veterans, we just jumped a little, slammed the trunk shut, and hurried into the house. "But it wasn't firecrackers, was it?" he asked. We all trooped out to the street, and took a closer look at the car. There it was—a bullet-size gash.

With a little more street reporting, we figured out the mystery. At exactly the same moment Steve picked the cello up and slung it over his shoulder, there was a brief gunfight—not firecrackers—in the vestibule of the house next door. A stray bullet flew out, hit the car, then ricocheted off the trunk and into Steve's cello, which was shielding his hip and back. He could have been killed.

When we came back into the house, sobered and shaky, Steve looked down at his lovely but wounded instrument. "This is the cello that saved my ass," he said, with equal parts wonder and gratitude.

Small Craft Warning

Over the years, I had never really given up my dream of having another child, and in that long-held dream, the child I always saw was a little girl. But like most women, I had been taught to believe that I had to be in a committed relationship with a man who shared that dream before it could become a reality.

Brian was out of the picture, however, and dating, such as it was, ran the gamut from awkward to uncomfortable to hugely weird. When a friend suggested that I put a personal ad in *New York* magazine, I figured, oh, what the heck. And then the huge manila envelopes full of replies started coming through the mail slot. The boys would carefully screen the letters and pictures inside, making stacks of the ones who looked okay and the ones whose pictures probably belonged on "Most Wanted" flyers in the post office.

When a date arrived, Nick and Lexi always answered the door, and by the time I came downstairs they were ready to vote: thumbs up, thumbs down. In the worst cases, their eyes would roll; they wanted the rejects out the door before the date had even begun. I have to give them credit—they were almost always right.

All in all, I had some uncomfortable experiences and I made some new friends, but the girl who held her breath waiting for Prince Charming all those years ago was definitely gone, replaced now by an adult woman with two teenage boys, one mortgage, and a job that took all I had to give it—and returned more than I ever could have asked for. The simple truth: Remarriage was not in my immediate future.

But did that mean that I couldn't—or shouldn't— have another child, I wondered? Why? I was around children all day long, including the two I was raising, and I wasn't intimidated by the thought of a third. I lived in a community where children were part of the dynamic—my colleagues taught my kids and I taught theirs. The boys were still young enough to be active brothers to anyone who might join our family, and when it came time for them to go off to college, a third child would still need the part of me I valued the most—the mother part. I decided to investigate the possibilities of adoption.

Early in the process, one reputable agency in New

York ruled me out as a prospective adoptive parent due to my age (approaching forty), my unmarried status, and my two healthy children. I received similar responses from other organizations. The more I was turned away, the more determined I became to find a child.

One of my CPE parents had adopted a child from Honduras, and recommended that I speak with the social worker who had helped her out. When I called her (the woman's name was Miriam), she was immediately receptive and full of information. She outlined the steps I'd have to go through in the adoption process: the psychological study, the home study, the background checks, the paperwork that the Immigration and Naturalization Service required for adopting children from other countries. It sounded daunting, but not impossible. She also recommended a number of contacts in South America and Mexico; eventually we settled on one in El Salvador.

Initially, the boys' response was mixed. Nick worried that I was only reacting to the empty nest in my future, and that I would be limiting any social opportunities that I might have once he and Lexi were out of the house. In a way, he almost played devil's advocate, forcing me to rethink all my reasoning in order to respond to his questions. Lexi, however, loved the idea immediately. "We have to do this, Mom," he said. "We have to." In the end, they both agreed—they would support me in any way they could, and they would welcome, with open arms, any child who came in through our front door to be part of our family.

Throughout the preliminaries, I had so many phone conversations with Miriam the social worker that I felt as though we'd become friends. She always gave me wise and caring advice. She had adopted, too, she told me—a mixed-race child from Vietnam whose dad had been an American soldier.

The afternoon Miriam was scheduled to visit us for the home study, I was a nervous wreck. I had vacuumed and scrubbed and polished every visible inch of the house, and I shampooed the dog until she was probably convinced her skin was coming off. I cleaned in places no social worker ever would have seen, and then did it all over again. Of course, it was complete torture for my sons. I barely allowed them to breathe in their own rooms, to open the refrigerator, to touch a single surface.

When we all got home from school that afternoon, I made the boys take baths, iron some clean clothes, and sit—"Don't move!"—on the couch, which is where the three of us were perched nervously when the doorbell rang. I went to the door, and there stood a woman and a man. Miriam introduced herself, and the gentleman (who was carrying a laptop computer) helped her in through the door. We watched with uncertainty and then with astonishment as she gingerly felt for the edges of the couch and lowered herself onto the cushions, arranging the laptop near her. Nick, Lexi and I looked at each other in silent amazement: Miriam was blind.

Nick glanced down at his clothes, a clean, freshly

ironed shirt and pants with a knife-edge crease down the front. He looked at me, shaking his head, the beginning of a smile forming on his lips.

Within minutes of setting up the laptop, Miriam began to ask us incisive and often extremely personal questions. As eager as I was to adopt, it was hard at first to be relaxed or candid in my answers, and the boys were struggling with this, too. Were there right answers and wrong ones? Would one wrong word rule out our chances? Should we worry about what she needed to hear versus what was true for us? However, Miriam's own candor and personality put us all at ease; it was clear that she wanted what was best for a child who at that very moment may have been waiting for a home.

Although I had said that the best situation for me would be an older child, at least four (school-age, so I could continue to work during the day), Miriam quickly decided that an infant would be better for our household. With sports and music, with school and my teaching schedule, and kids trooping in and out for private lessons, our days were scheduled down to the minute. "An older child often has trouble fitting into someone else's established routine," she told us. "The routine would have to adjust for that child—whereas babies simply become part of whatever activity is going on around them."

A baby? Crying? Teething? Feedings every four hours? "Yes, that's a tough time of adjustment, but it's over fairly quickly," Miriam reminded me, and as I looked at the two large boys next to me, I had to agree with her. Those early days go by in a hurry. OK, then, it was decided: We were having a baby.

Almost two years later, the boys and I found out that there was indeed an actual baby on the way, due in February of 1991. If everything went according to plan, we might have the newest member of our family in late spring, perhaps in June.

For the next few months, I often found myself day-dreaming in the middle of a violin class, or while making lasagne, or simply while walking down the street. I didn't put on weight, I didn't have to buy maternity clothes, but for all practical purposes, I was pregnant.

After that year's December break, I walked into the beginners' class ready to bring them back down to earth from the holiday frenzy, and I noticed immediately that very few of the kids had their violins. "Hey, what's going on with you guys?" I asked, annoyed that my plans for class were now moot. "How could you come to class and not remember to bring your violins with you?"

They all looked hesitantly at each other, shifting nervously from one foot to the other the way little kids do. "Well," piped one, "we heard you got fired."

"What?" I said. "That's the silliest thing I ever heard."

One of the girls shook her head. "But my parents said it was in the newsletter, Roberta. Something about a budget, or no money, or something like that. Anyway, you got fired."

Since Nick and Lexi were no longer in the elementary school, the CPE newsletter didn't automatically come home in the boys' backpacks anymore; I often had to remind myself to pick it up so that I could keep up with what was going on. The problem with trooping back and forth among three buildings with a loaded car and a backpack full of violins, of course, was that keeping informed was exactly the thing I never found time to do.

In a state of panic, I ran down the hall and burst into the office of the director, Lucy Matos. "Is it true?" I gasped. Lucy was a longtime friend and supporter, a trusted colleague, and, I suspect, a very bad poker player—the truth was written all over her face. "It's true," she said grimly. "The violin program has been cut. I'm so sorry that I couldn't get to you before the news did, Roberta—I was trying to rally the parents with the newsletter first, and with the holiday break, the lines of communication got crossed."

The city, like much of the Northeast, was deep in the throes of a recession, and the Board of Education cuts, which had been announced over the break, were painfully deep from one end of the system to the other. For all intents and purposes, the violin program was over.

"But can't we fight? Isn't there something we can do?" *What about the violin kids?* I thought. Almost 150 of them. *And what about my own kids?* And then I remembered—oh, my God, we had a baby on the way!

I wanted someone to be angry with, someone to blame, and someone to fight with, but clearly it wasn't Lucy—or, for that matter, Debbie Meier. The checkbook, and the final decision, rested with the Board of Ed, and the decision was evidently final.

Stunned, I walked back into the hall. The beginners with no violins were sent back to their regular classrooms, but other kids showed up throughout the day with violins in hand, expecting a lesson. So I tried to teach, but it was halfhearted or worse; I couldn't shake the sensation that the breath had gone out of my body.

In my mind, I went over and over the past weeks and months—more than a decade, in fact. There had been no signs that funding for the program had ever been at risk, no indication that the value of the program itself had ever been in question. Many of our kids were good enough to belong to outside orchestras; the city's InterSchool Orchestras had accepted a number of them over the previous years, offering them scholarships; still others had been accepted into the Juilliard Music Advancement Program. The concerts, in both attendance and performance, were major community events each year, swelling the number of parents and kids vying for the following year's lottery. The responses were always the same: "This music, these kids—it's unbelievable!" If anything, we should have been looking for ways to expand.

Once again, I thought, I've been wiped out by a disaster I never saw coming. If I had seen one clue, maybe

I could've figured out some sort of preemptive or protective move. But it was too late.

When Nick and Lexi got home late that afternoon, I was sitting at the kitchen table with a glass of wine, my eyes swollen. "What is it?" Nick asked tensely—he probably thought someone was hurt, or dead.

"Budget cuts," I told them. "The violin program is cut. We only have until June, and then it's over."

"What?" they cried. "They can't do that to you!"

"Well," I said, my voice shaking, "they just did."

"But they can't!" Nick said, beginning to pace around the room, his fists clenched though he wanted to hit someone. "To end it, just like that? It's completely crazy!"

Lexi had a stunned look on his face. "But, Mom," he asked, "don't they care about all those kids, and the wonderful concerts? What will happen to everybody now?"

Realistically, I wasn't out of choices. I had made friends and colleagues throughout New York's music world, and I had a good reputation as a teacher. In fact, I'd received the occasional job offer, from colleges and prep schools, but I had never really considered anything seriously—because this was my place, mine and my sons'.

"I don't want to run away, I don't want to teach at some fancy private school," I said. "But I don't know what to do."

Nick was on one side of me, Lexi was on the other,

their arms wrapped around my shoulders. "Fight back," they said, almost in unison. "Come on, Mom—we have to fight back."

The phone was ringing off the hook—parents of students. Dani Toomer, a fellow teacher, one of my oldest friends at CPE—her son Omari had been one of my first students. Ellen Weiss, dear friend and mother of Nora Friedman, whose passionate playing always reminded me of myself at that age. Barry Crumbley—I would teach violin to four of his kids. Jean Horton—I would teach all three of hers.

"Come on, Roberta," they all said. "This can't happen. We have to fight back."

The previous summer, at the Bennington Music Conference, I had become friends with a man named Ed Miller, who played the viola. In addition to being a musician, Ed, whose undergraduate degree was in music composition, was working on his master's degree at the Harvard Graduate School of Education. Although he lived near Boston, he had often come to New York to observe the violin classes, and decided to use some of what he saw in the research project that would ultimately become his master's thesis.

When Ed heard that the violin program had been eliminated—and that we were trying to draw up a battle plan—he talked to his faculty adviser and thesis committee, and came up with an ingenious idea: Why not have the subject of his thesis actually be the saving of the program?

The idea seemed overwhelming at first, but we needed only a few kitchen-table sessions before it began to take realistic shape. After all, the program had more than proven its worth to the community; the only question was how to pay for it. The answer: We'd pay for it ourselves. We would raise enough money to compensate for the budget cuts, work out some kind of compromise relationship with the Board of Education, hope that the city's financial mess would ultimately resolve itself—and in the meantime, the violin program would stay right where it was.

I went to Debbie Meier to let her know what we were going to try to do. As frustrated and scared as I was about my position, I didn't envy hers—she had always vowed to "maintain the mindset of a teacher rather than an administrator," and now here she was, on the other side of the desk, charged with representing the bureaucracy in the wake of a fiscal crisis. It was everything she abhorred, and it threatened to undermine everything she believed in and had fought for at CPE.

"I can't stop you and I can't support you and I can't advise you," she said, choosing her words very carefully and giving me the clear-eyed, straightforward look that had grown familiar to me over the years. Implicit in what she did not say were the same words I'd heard the first day we met: "Go for it."

While Ed Miller's Harvard connections were impressive, it was actually his old high-school friends (from Teaneck, New Jersey) who proved to be our first team of guardian angels. His best friend, Dan Soyer, was the son of David Soyer, the cellist from the esteemed Guarneri String Quartet; another friend was connected to the editor of the Metropolitan section of the *New York Times*; yet another was affiliated with ABC-TV's news magazine, *Primetime Live*. Almost before I knew it, we had a *Times* reporter, Evelyn Nieves, at school; an ABC film crew taping the violin kids in class; and David Soyer and his lovely wife, Janet, sitting in my kitchen for Sunday brunch.

After we explained the nature of the budget crisis and showed a video of one of the end-of-the-year violin concerts (and after Nick took advantage of the circumstances to play the cello), David Soyer generously volunteered the contents of his Rolodex, which contained the names, addresses, and phone numbers of classical musicians from one end of the country (of the world, really) to the other. At that point, the Guarneri Quartet had been together a quarter of a century; the information in that Rolodex was as priceless as any Stradivarius.

Ed Miller drafted a straightforward but moving letter, explaining who I was, what the East Harlem Violin Program was, and what was about to happen to it. "Come to our school, come to a class," we pleaded. "Just come and hear these kids and help us save this violin program." In order to take donations, we began the process of setting up a nonprofit foundation, to be called the Opus 118 Music Center, after the street my house is on.

A few weeks later, Evelyn Nieves's article appeared on the front page of the *Times* Metro section, and it was more than I could have hoped for—generous, factually correct (I came to really appreciate this as the weeks went by), and with great pictures of the kids and me in violin class. And right behind her came a local television reporter, Morry Alter from CBS, channel 2. We were all so proud when Morry turned to the camera just as the kids started to play, and whispered, "This is where the reporter gets his socks knocked off!" At the bottom of the screen, the TV station listed my home phone number.

One afternoon soon afterward, I picked up the phone and was greeted with a heavily accented (Russian), Old World voice. "You don't know me," the gentleman said, "but my name is Alexander Schneider."

"Oh, yes, I do know you," I said. Alexander Schneider, then in his late seventies, was the second violinist of the legendary Budapest Quartet, and he was a beloved icon in the music world.

"Who do I make the check out to?" he asked. That the esteemed "Sascha," as he was called (but not by me, certainly) should be our first donor struck me as an auspicious sign.

During the Christmas season of 1992, Nick was

lucky enough to work with Schneider in the New York String Seminar, and play three concerts with him—two at Carnegie Hall, one at the Kennedy Center. Sadly, Schneider died soon after, in March of 1993, but his gift of seed money lives on in Opus 118, and in the kids.

One of the first lessons of a not-for-profit organization is that when you take money from people, you are now, for all intents and purposes, identified with those donors. Perception in the community is vitally important—anything that can be misinterpreted can have a backlash effect, reducing your credibility, weakening whatever your mission is, and causing people whose trust you need to look at you with suspicion.

Early on, Opus 118 received a donation of $1,000 from Minister Louis Farrakhan, and we experienced what I can only call a Deborah Meier moment—an organization full of passionate people, sharing one mission, but with at least a dozen different life experiences and cultures they bring to that mission. Many of the African-Americans saw Farrakhan as a force for good in the black community, but there was the thorny issue of his being on the record as anti-Semitic. We returned the donation. We were later offered a sizeable donation by a big tobacco company, but refused that as well.

Morry Alter's television piece ran in the New York metropolitan area at least four times over that Mother's Day weekend. On Sunday morning, as I was taking advantage of a lull in the action to do some laundry, the telephone rang yet again. This time it was a big resonant basso voice. "Hullo!" it boomed. "Roberta? This is It-zhak Perlman!"

This was the unlikely equivalent of Nick and Lexi hearing from Mickey Mantle while they were in Little League. I immediately took the receiver away from my ear and looked at it. "Itzhak!" I blurted. "I mean, Mr. Perlman!"

"I came home from a concert last night, turned on the news, and saw your kids on TV. They sounded terrific! What can I do to help?"

I don't think I've ever heard so much energy in one voice. Once I got over the shock, I managed to give him a few details. Mid-conversation, he realized he had received the letter from us, courtesy of David Soyer's mailing list; apologetically, he admitted it was buried somewhere in a pile of papers on his desk. I knew the *Primetime Live* piece was going to run quite soon, with many scenes of the kids playing, and promised to get him a copy. And then I asked him to come to our end-of-the-year concert in June. "I'll be there," he promised.

After I hung up, I couldn't quite believe what had just happened. *Happy Mother's Day to me,* I thought.

A few days later, with a cash advance on my Mastercard, I wired money to El Salvador—the baby was on her way. She would arrive in New York on June 26, two days after what could have been the violin program's last concert.

Lifeline

"People have learned that they may not be rich, they may not be politically connected, but that they do have a voice—and they can make things happen."
—SUSANA ALMANZA, *1998 Petra Fellow*

*O*ur preparations for the end-of-the-year concert usu-*ally begin in April,* right after spring break. As the time grows closer, the excitement level begins to climb. Rehearsals start accumulating—a weeknight here, a Saturday there. There's always a lot of anxiety, but it's equally balanced with joy.

In 1991, however, there was a third emotion: fear. We were under the gun, and everybody knew it. We also had a glimmer of hope: We had already raised almost $40,000, with pledges of more to come—we knew we were safe for at least one more year, thanks to parents and teachers and so many others I didn't even know whose envelopes just kept coming. I felt overwhelmed by the response, and deeply grateful for it. However, it was my first lesson in saying "Thank you" at the very moment I was thinking, *Oh, dear—I'm afraid this isn't enough.* Would we be able to work out a relationship with the Board of Ed and with the district? Could we get past the first awkward arrangements and the tension, and create a plan that would work for everyone?

Although we all hoped that Itzhak Perlman would attend the concert, I couldn't be sure if he would actually be able to do it, so I hadn't told the kids or the parents that we might have a distinguished guest. And then, just a few minutes before I was ready to march the kids from the gym into the auditorium, Nick came running in and whispered to me, "He's here, Mom! Itzhak came!" He was in the audience with his wife, Tobey, also a professional violinist.

There were 120 kids on that un–air-conditioned stage that day, including ten graduates, and even the youngest ones knew how important the moment was for all of us. I wanted the audience to understand, and see, and care about what the community would lose if this program disappeared. I always tell the kids to play with all their heart, but this time they instinctively knew, and gave the performance of their lives.

Ever since the first concert, the tradition has been to begin with the entire group, all ages, playing "Twinkle" variations. The older kids stand behind the little ones, who are in rows in front of the stage—at this point, I've convinced them that I can see each and every one of them from where I'm standing with my own violin, about halfway up the aisle in the audience. They're so precise, with their feet planted in just the right way, their scrolls and their noses aimed at me, their bellies facing to my left, and their bows all coming off the strings at the same time. Their eyes grow wider and wider as the music builds around them—I can see them taking bigger breaths as they realize they're part of the sound the whole group is making. No matter how sophisticated the music becomes as the concert goes on, there's something about those first few minutes that crystallizes the power that each child has.

For weeks, Nick, Lexi, and I had rehearsed the slow movement of Mendelssohn's Trio in D Minor. A beautiful lullaby—_andante con moto tranquillo_—it is tender and moving, much like a love song. We thought of it as our family's farewell gift to the people we truly loved and the community we'd fought so hard to belong to. I knew that with all the other memories, this would be one of the most bittersweet. Once we'd begun, I didn't want it to end.

The showpiece for the evening was Bach's Third Brandenburg Concerto, and not the abridged version, either—the whole thing. The kids played with so much spirit and joy, I was beaming with pride. After the concert, when I went up to Itzhak and thanked him and his wife for coming, he praised the performance. "Your kids make such a beautiful sound!" he said. "And you're talking to _two_ professional violinists here; Tobey and I are so impressed!"

Our tradition has always been to end the concert

with *We Shall Overcome*. Once we started playing, the audience gradually began to sing, softly at first, then swelling to a full crescendo. Everywhere I looked, people were wiping away tears. Suddenly, I knew that we could make it work.

Smiling, Itzhak stood up from his place in the audience, and to my utter surprise walked slowly to the front of the auditorium. The audience leaped to their feet and began to applaud wildly, the kids cheering and stomping and whistling like he was a rock star or Michael Jordan. Then he spoke to us all.

First, I want to say to the boys and girls who played in tonight's concert that the music was absolutely terrific. Bravo! Tonight, indeed, the music speaks for itself. But we should not relax. We cannot stop fighting for this program, and others like it. My own experience with five children has taught me that all too much education deals with the learning of facts and procedures. It's the rare class that actually improves one's ability to think. The violin program does just that—it teaches hard work, discipline, and the ability to attain a goal. These are invaluable skills that regardless of fiscal circumstances should not be sacrificed. And a teacher with the enthusiasm and dedication of Roberta cannot be sacrificed, either.

There are two ways to look at an evening such as this. A shortsighted thinker might say that this was all so wonderful, but we simply do not have the money to fund such a luxury—sorry, kids. I would tell that thinker that hard work and discipline are no luxury, that a program such as this gives our children the very skills necessary to cope with problems of the future, and with college, and such skills produce not just violinists, but doctors and lawyers as well. This program also teaches that the foundation for excellence is perseverance.

The baby was escorted from El Salvador to Florida by the Salvadoran attorney I had been working with and his wife. My sister Lois was scheduled to meet them in Miami and then bring the baby to New York. All that day, I watched the clock and paced from garden to kitchen to front door, and watched the clock some more. And then the phone rang. It was Lois, in Miami. "Bert, I'm at the airport, and I've got her!" she announced. "I've got good and bad news."

My heart fell. "What is it?"

"Well, the good news is, she's gorgeous," Lois said. "The bad news is, I may not be able to give her up!"

A joke, I thought. I'm going to have a heart attack from my sister's joke.

Lexi and I drove to the airport, holding the two snapshots the agency had sent us—Nick was already at Greenwood Music Camp, waiting for us to visit with the baby the following weekend. The plane was already on the ground when we got to the airport, and we ran to the gate, desperately looking for Lois. When we finally spotted her, with the baby in her arms, we all burst into tears. Ever since, Lois has always thought of herself as the Stork.

"I can't believe it," Lexi kept saying. "She's a miracle. This is a miracle." Sophia Estefania, my daughter, four months old—large, dark eyes in a tiny little self, curled in my arms as though she'd always been there. We could not stop looking at her—the delicate long fingers, the thick black hair. She looked back at us with a level gaze as though she knew us—as though to say, *Hola, mi familia.*

In many households, a new baby creates complete upheaval—busy days, sleepless nights. But in my house, so much had happened in the months before Sophia's arrival that caring for her that first summer gave me a way to become centered again, with time to reflect on everything that had gone on. All I had to do was read the letters from parents and supporters, and go through the newspaper clippings and videotapes that chronicled the struggles of the East Harlem Violin Program.

Some of the television coverage was wonderful, focusing primarily on the kids and giving them plenty of time not only to play, but to talk about what the music meant to them. In addition, it seemed to open up the whole subject of what was going on in the schools, and how we were going to cope with the cuts to arts education.

However, it seemed to me that many of the reporters hadn't spent much time in East Harlem. One crew wanted to film me walking across First Avenue with the reporter—not so much to see me doing it, I suspected, as to show the poor, pathetic neighborhood. As we crossed 118th Street and grew nearer to Patsy's Pizzeria, raw eggs came raining down from the roof of the building next door and splattered onto the videocams. We got out of there fast. Later, when another network wanted to take a walk around, I talked them out of it.

Primetime Live was in many ways the most troubling. The first words you heard were: "Harlem . . . tough streets, hard times, broken-down neighborhoods." They played ominous gangster rap in the background as their camera filmed an abandoned lot filled with garbage, behind a broken fence. Why not Jefferson Park, I wondered, with its green grass, perfectly healthy fence, and families with baby carriages? Why not the shops along La Marqueta, with the salsa music coming out of doorways making you want to attempt a samba down the sidewalk?

The first fact they gave about one of my students, Melia Crumbley, was to describe her as the child of divorced parents. As a divorced parent myself, I thought, *wait just a minute*: This was not a Dickensian novel—this was 1991, and this talented girl had always had the great mutual support of her parents for her music; her father, Barry, has been a stalwart member of Opus's board since the very beginning. Here's a partial text of the voiceover as Melia was shown coming out of her apartment with her younger sister: "They come from broken homes, through graffiti'd streets, carrying their violins like passports to a better future." Believe me, that didn't make her life easier that week, nor mine either.

The kids in my neighborhood have the same aspirations and the same dreams as kids in any part of this country have. Music is *not* a way out of this neighborhood; it's a way into their souls.

On the other hand, I did get a kick out of hearing Ellen Weiss, Nora's mom and my dear friend, saying, "Roberta will do anything to get the kids to do better. She'll use every down-and-dirty trick she can get her hands on." *You bet I will,* I thought.

So often, reporters come into Harlem—or its urban equivalents in America's cities—with a preconceived take on the situation: Look at the poor, struggling ghetto peasants. They lead with the divorced and single-parent statistics, or the welfare numbers, and they push a viewer or reader to lazy-thinking assumptions that often have little to do with what goes on inside those apartments. We forget: Those are homes. Families live in them.

In our case, using a zoom lens, they zoomed in through the broken window of an abandoned building, and then they pulled back; then they zoomed again, this time into a gathering of beautifully dressed kids, surrounded by light, playing "Oh, Come Little Children" like angels—*diminuendo*, then *crescendo*—leaving the viewer with the impression that by teaching violin, I had lifted them out of the abandoned building into the heavens.

Of all the press coverage, I most appreciated Tom Brokaw's comments. The violin program, he said, was a "metaphor for how urban life should work: people of all races doing something difficult together—making music." He stressed the importance of the self-esteem factor, and for the basketball-addled kids who think the only way to raise themselves up is to play in the NBA, Brokaw said, as I always do, that the violin program is "another way to get to play at Madison Square Garden."

During the school year, I received another miraculous telephone call, this time from Arnold Steinhardt, the first violinist of the Guarneri String Quartet. Arnold expressed his great concern over the state of music education for kids, and asked if he might come and hear the kids play. I was thrilled to extend the invitation.

The day Arnold arrived, I had assembled all the kids, beginners through sixth grade, in the basement of CPE1. I had explained to them who was coming, and they were so excited—a man who played 150 concerts a year was coming to see us play the violin! Not one child dropped an instrument, tied a shoe, poked a neighbor with a bow, or asked to go to the bathroom—and they all played beautifully. I felt so proud, and blessed; as it turned out, I was.

He had come, Arnold told me, not only to hear the kids—whom he pronounced "miraculous"—but to do a little research. He had been thinking of nominating me for an "unsung heroes" award from the Petra Foundation; once he heard the kids play, he was convinced.

The foundation was established in memory of Petra Tölle Shattuck (a dear friend of Arnold's wife, Dorothea von Haeften), who had died tragically of a brain hemorrhage just a few years before. Petra, who taught at Harvard, was a passionate human rights advocate, and her husband, John Shattuck (now the ambassador to the Czech Republic) had set up the foundation "recognizing unsung individuals who lift barriers and free the spirit."

Our visitor had come across town in a cab, and when the class was over, I volunteered to drive him back to the West Side in the old Honda Civic. Arnold, whom I later discovered had a great appreciation for utilitarian vehicles (he has an ancient pickup truck), couldn't stop talking about my car. "It's silly to have anything in the city that doesn't do a job," he said. "The handling, the use of space. This is a great car."

I was still trying to get over the fact that he'd spent the entire morning listening to the violin kids. "I can't thank you enough for coming," I said. "When a famous musician reaches out to these kids and tells them they're good, it really psyches them up. They love it."

"No, Roberta, I thank *you*," he said. "It's easy for us professionals to forget where it all began for us. I went to public school, too—we need teachers like you."

Not long after that, Arnold's wife, Dorothea von Haeften, came to my house to photograph and interview me for the Petra Foundation, for I had indeed been voted a fellow of the foundation and granted a small stipend. Petra's gift, and the honor that came with it, opened the door to a wonderful organization, inviting me into a network of community activists and giving me even more support for speaking out about what mattered to me.

Dodo, as she is known to her friends, is a professional photographer, and how the world should look (as opposed to the way it does look) is a matter of passionate concern to her. Elegant and understated, she has an uncompromising integrity; Arnold often says he wouldn't ever want to be on the other side of a battle if Dodo was leading the charge. "I get emotionally caught up with things," he says, "and then I usually go back to practicing my violin. But Dodo puts on her armor and goes to work." It wasn't long before she joined the Opus 118 Board, and the two of them became stalwart champions of the East Harlem Violin Program.

"We need to get more publicity and more money," Dodo declared. "I think it's time for a benefit concert." She had recently organized a benefit concert with another friend—how hard, we thought, could it be to do another one? By now, it was the fall of 1992; the target date we decided to aim for was the following May. What she had in mind was something bigger than the end-of-the-year concert: she was picturing the violin kids in a major performance venue, an audience filled with patrons who could turn the fate of the program completely around. Not only that, but she was picturing Arnold, Itzhak Perlman, and anybody else she could persuade to be right up on that stage with the kids.

Dodo set up an appointment with a friend of hers named Walter Scheuer. He was a great patron of the arts, a philanthropist and documentary film producer, she told me. "We'll ask him to be the chairman of the benefit committee," she said. "He'll be perfect."

All these years later, I can find no other way to describe Wally Scheuer than as a true gift. When Dodo talked with him (and made sure he saw all the publicity material on the violin program), Wally had just created his not-for-profit Music for the World Foundation, whose purpose is to "address, and ideally correct, the decline in American music education." He promptly agreed to become chairman of the benefit committee, saying, "This is exactly right for us."

Wally, I discovered, wasn't just any documentary film producer. *From Mao to Mozart: Isaac Stern in China* won an Academy Award in 1981, and he had also produced *High Fidelity: The Adventures of the Guarneri String Quartet* in 1988. This past year there was another Oscar nomination, for *Dance Maker*, a documentary about choreographer Paul Taylor.

We initially hoped to schedule our concert for May of 1993, and quickly discovered that this was prime time for benefits—other people's benefits—with whom we couldn't hope to compete. We began to look to the fall instead. Dodo had been in touch with the 92nd

Street Y, and also with Town Hall and Lincoln Center, but we hadn't been able to get a definite commitment. However, at that year's end-of-the-year concert at CPE, we once again had an esteemed guest in our audience: maestro Isaac Stern.

"This," he said afterwards, gesturing at the violin kids as the applause and cheers rang through the room, "has to go to Carnegie Hall." What a lovely compliment, I thought—and then Dodo reminded me: Isaac Stern was the president of Carnegie's Board of Trustees. If he said we were going to Carnegie Hall, we were probably going to Carnegie Hall.

Wally Scheuer's director, Allan Miller, and his producer, Susan Kaplan, were also at the concert that day, filming the kids. When they went back to him with the footage, they all agreed it was much more than a concert: It was going to be the beginning of their next documentary.

Showtime!

" . . . not to make 'musicians' out of everyday performers, but more important, to make them educated, alert, caring, inquiring young people, who by
playing music feel a part of the connective tissue between what the mind of man has been able to devise
and the creativity of music . . . in other words, become literate, and part of the culture of the whole
world."

—ISAAC STERN

I tell the beginning violin kids that they must practice,
but I can never be completely sure what kind of
backup I'm getting at home. I have good relationships
with most of the parents, and they're enthusiastic in
their support, but there are ordinary distractions that
everybody overlooks once in a while. It might be the
TV, or loud music down the hall, or maybe a new baby
sharing the same bedroom. There must be patience and
tolerance for the young violinists' struggles in the beginning. There must be a quiet corner (and really, that's
all they need, a corner) where they can tape up their

music and concentrate for fifteen, twenty minutes at a time.

The best prescription, no matter what's going on at home, is to give them a regimen: Every day, do this three times. Make a written schedule, put it on the fridge or the bedroom wall, check it off every time you do it. Then I set a series of particular goals. The first major reward for the beginners comes when they're finally allowed to take their violins home, after about eight weeks of study with me. Later the incentives become even more attractive—the most enticing being the chance to play the national anthem at a New York Knicks game in Madison Square Garden.

"You've got three weeks to make it sound great," I tell them, and those kids focus like laser beams. For three weeks, they won't do anything but play that violin. Over and over, I've seen it happen, and I've heard it from their parents. "I don't know what happened to him all of a sudden," they say, shaking their heads. Well, I know.

We've gone to Madison Square Garden every year since 1993; this past spring, it was for one of the NBA playoff games. It's always an amazing experience—there we are in a sports arena with the wildest, noisiest sports fans in the world. They give us fifty tickets, and I take as many kids as I can squeeze in. We have a half hour for the sound check, and we're out there adjusting microphones, choreographing getting on and off the court as quickly as possible, while both teams are warming up, running up and down and firing basketballs. The kids are beside themselves with excitement, craning their necks at these giant athletes, and they grin with a kind of frozen terror when we actually march out on the court to play. Many times, the crowd snickers. "Who are these little twerps with the violins?" But as the first notes of the anthem drift out over the basketball court, the crowd immediately hushes. A popcorn vendor once told us that while we're out there, you can hear a pin drop from anyplace in the Garden; another employee says that it's the only time all season that the crowd lets the performers get to the last note—usually they're cheering before it's over, just to get the game started. But when we play the anthem, they really listen. And *then* the cheering comes, and it's for us.

When we come off the floor, everyone from Patrick Ewing to Spike Lee high-fives the kids, and so do the fans surrounding us where we settle in to watch the game. "Want to play on an NBA court?" I tease the kids. "You just did."

The unfortunate thing about this is that although the games are always televised, we perform during the first commercial break, and the rest of America never sees the evidence of what these kids can do—city kids, kids of color, boys and girls from eight to eighteen, playing the violin and bringing down the house.

When Arnold Steinhardt asked Wally Scheuer, during the filming of the *High Fidelity* documentary, why he was putting such a heart-and-soul effort into a documentary about music, about classical musicians—something that would likely make little or no money—Wally told him, "I want to make a few footprints in the sand before I leave this world." I suspect he didn't expect the landscape to be as complicated to navigate as it was in East Harlem.

Making a documentary film that involves teachers and children, public-school facilities, and bureaucratic headaches, must be a little like organizing a military invasion, only without the benefit of a Pentagon budget. When you're trying to do it in New York City, the headaches, potential and real, are at least ten times as big.

To begin with, I had so many reservations and fears. I didn't even like having my own picture taken; how would I feel about a camera being in the room when I needed to reprimand a kid or make an uncomfortable decision? And how would that kid feel? Were the filmmakers planning on recording everything we did? And then would they use it all? Would it make me censor myself? Would I be able to teach as I had always done, or would I be so self-conscious that I wouldn't be able to give the kids what they needed?

Ultimately, I decided that the most important thing was the violin program, and what the Carnegie Hall concert would mean for us and our survival. We had to be focused, we had to be great, and all our energy had to go into the intense rehearsals, into the music itself. In order for that to happen, my anxieties about the documentary had to be set aside. I needed to concentrate only on the work we had ahead of us—how I looked or sounded while we were doing that didn't matter.

Understandably, there were some teachers and staff who had already suffered through the barrage of media publicity about the violin program—they'd simply had enough. "The violin kids are really getting swelled heads," someone said. School was for learning, not for movie-making. Children and teachers deal with plenty of distractions already—a camera crew roaming through the halls for the entire school year was asking too much. And what about kids who weren't in the violin program? Would this undercut the school's whole sense of community?

Fortunately, Susan Kaplan and Allan Miller were very aware of the objections and concerns. Diplomatic and patient, they worked hard to build bridges, mediating as fairly as they could on behalf of everyone. Each day, disputes had to be resolved and balance had to be restored—and each day, Susan and Allan did that.

When the first preparations for the Carnegie Hall concert were being made, an acquaintance of Dodo's who is a professional in the fund-raising business compared the project to "a bunch of housewives running a lemonade stand." But as the actual date approached, it became clearer to everyone that something big was about to happen.

Almost every professional musician Arnold and

Dodo contacted wanted to participate with us in some way. Given the diversity of both the kids and the audience, they felt it was only good sense, and appropriate, to have artists of color at the concert. They wanted the performers to be string players; after all, the benefit was to be a celebration of the violin. But it was also about the kids, their different cultures and traditions—the concert needed to reflect the true face of the community. Just think of that name Carnegie, and the libraries he built so that all people would have access to literacy and culture.

That's when they suggested bringing in jazz musicians like John Blake Jr., Diane Monroe, and Karen Briggs, and Mark O'Connor, the fabulous bluegrass fiddler who's been nominated for many Grammy awards. Dodo reported that there were a few raised eyebrows at that, and some strong objections from . . . well, let's call them classicists, or maybe purists, concerned about diluting the quality of the program. Apparently, there was a somewhat heated meeting about this, and then Isaac Stern said, "When I was young, we used to go to hear jazz performers live all the time—Miles Davis, Oscar Peterson. It was great music." That clinched it for everyone.

Arnold and I met a couple of times to discuss the concert repertoire and figure out how the program should be organized. What music would the kids play? What pieces would the artists perform? And what could they perform together? Slowly, a magical evening was taking shape.

In the meantime, the violin kids and I had our own work cut out for us. To allow for extra rehearsals, I drew up a contract for the parents, in which I asked them to make a commitment that their kids would attend all rehearsals, right up to the concert. Students with other extracurricular activities had to make choices, and some of them were very difficult. The concert would pull in students from all three schools, plus graduates. I carefully went over the list, trying to select those violinists whom I knew would be excellent. I also chose kids who, although they weren't stars, were doing good work—an experience like this would encourage them to grow.

Just before school was to start that fall, the headlines broke: A citywide asbestos crisis was going to delay all school openings. For most parents and students in New York, it was dismaying news; for us, it was another example of a crisis turning to our favor, since it gave us ten days of solid rehearsal time during what normally would have been school time. This was a wonderful way to foster a bonding in the group. We rehearsed in the Leiderkranz Building on the Upper East Side, where the InterSchool Orchestras meet, and from the very first day I pushed them, hard. The documentary cameras were running the whole time, and every word I said—or shouted—was miked; every move we made, even the bad ones, was caught on film.

The grand finale was going to be the Bach Double Concerto. I couldn't believe it—fourteen of my students, each sharing a music stand with a famous violinist, and I would be in front of all those guys, leading them! Every time the reality of that hit me, I pushed it away. I couldn't think about it; I had to do it.

Somewhere in all the hoopla, it dawned on me that I needed to get a dress. But how to find the time? And how could I afford something special enough to wear on the stage of Carnegie Hall? And then my lovely cousin Sandy Guaspari-Rosenthal called me and announced, "Roberta, we're going shopping!" In one breathless day, the two of us hiked from one end of Madison Avenue to the other, determined to find the perfect dress. By the end of that day, I was exhausted and disillusioned; clearly, none of these high-fashion designers had me in mind when they were conjuring up their collections. And then we found it: simple black velvet, as soft and delicate as anything I had ever worn. As I was pulling out my credit card, Sandy stopped me. "No," she said. "This is my gift."

In the meantime, back at 118th Street, chaos was beginning to reign. By train, by bus, by plane, and by car, my entire family was coming into town. Mom and her companion, Frank; my brother Dougie, his wife, Pam, their son David; my father's brother Harry, his wife, Antoinette, and their son David; my sister, Lois, and my brother, Al. And that was just the immediate family; after that came the rest of the cousins. It was the first time everybody had been together since the last family wedding, almost twenty years before. There were wall-to-wall sleeping bags and mattresses on the floor; at one point, I thought we were going to have to draw straws for the bathroom. In the middle of it all, there was Sophia toddling from grown-up to grown-up.

For days in advance, I walked and drove all over town accumulating food: smoked mozzarella, proscuitto bread, sharp provolone, roasted red peppers, different kinds of olives, nuts, grapes, cases of wine and beer. Nick and Lexi pleaded with me—"Please, Mom, no baking, you'll be up until dawn!" I got away with it one night, and made several stacks of *pizzelles*, but after that I cheated and bought a huge tray of Italian cookies.

Wally Scheuer had promised to send some cars to the house to pick up the whole family and take us to Carnegie, but I was not prepared for what I saw when I looked out the window: a large group of people gathering in front of my house. "Lexi, what are all those people looking at out there?" I asked.

"Three stretch limos, Mom," Lexi proudly announced, "and I think they're for us!" Sure enough, there were two black limos and one white one, each seemingly the length of the house, lined up and waiting next to the curb, a half hour ahead of schedule. "But I'm not ready to go yet!" I wailed.

He smiled. "Mom, I think they'll wait for you."

By the time we actually left the house, we had to make our way through a huge crowd, excitedly waiting to see what famous people were going to get into those limos. "Oh, it's just the violin lady," said one of my neighbors, a little disappointed. As a driver helped me and my mother into our limo, I noticed that my two brothers were excitedly snapping pictures of the people and the limos and the drama that was unfolding before us.

Even the most seasoned professionals will tell you that Carnegie Hall always has a kind of "temple" feeling to it for a performer, no matter how often you play there. I'd gone to many concerts there and had often wondered what it would feel like to be on that stage. Now, I was about to find out.

Backstage, there were people walking around with headphones, counting down the minutes until curtain time. All around me I saw beautiful faces, the girls in satin dresses, the boys in dark suits and ties, each of them radiant with anticipation. I looked at the faces of these kids that I had known for so long, whose eyes were shining, whose parents and grandparents and brothers and sisters were sitting out in the audience, waiting. They had all worked so hard to get here. In all the weeks before, I had never told the kids what I knew with absolute certainty—this concert, and their performance, would be spectacular. It was time now to give them what they deserved to hear. "I would like you to play with all your hearts," I told them. "Play like I know you can play, and you'll be wonderful. Watch me, don't look out in the audience—you don't need to be afraid.

You'll be great, really wonderful." And then I put my hand over my pounding heart. "Play from *here*," I said.

The kids were given the signal to file out (we had been instructed to walk quickly), and I could hear the applause swelling as the audience greeted them. Once they were in position, it was my turn to go. For days, the tension and fear had been building in me. I took a deep breath, walked confidently to the front of the stage—and the fear was gone. It felt as though I had stepped into another world, and someone had extended his hand to guide me. Carnegie's seats are red; the lights in the hall are golden; everything was glowing. The audience was embracing us, and nothing could go wrong.

It went by in a dream. And when it was over, when we had played the last notes of the Bach Double finale, there was a moment of suspended silence—and then Carnegie Hall erupted. The sound continued for a very long time. As we all stood on the stage, bowing and crying for joy, there was wave after wave of thunderous applause. Our master of ceremonies, Billy Taylor, could not get the audience to stop.

"The kind of joy that emanated from both sides of the footlights was unprecedented in my experience," Arnold Steinhardt told me later. "The symbolism on the stage was so enormous, it was hard to know who was more inspired, the pros or the kids. In my lifetime, there have only been two concerts where I experienced this kind of emotion—and the other one was when Vladimir

Horowitz returned to the Carnegie stage after ten years."

It was so moving to see the response to what had just happened; these children had taken wing before our very eyes. The high, the exhilaration—it was past anything realistic, it felt like we were all going up to heaven via Carnegie Hall! That synergy, that joy, is the very best of what art can be.

Since that night, we have held a Fiddlefest concert every couple of years, although not at Carnegie. Many artists have generously shown up for us in other places at other times—Arnold, Isaac Stern, violinists Pamela Frank and Diane Monroe, were all able to join us at Fiddlefest in Zurich, when we played *We Shall Over-come* with forty Swiss kids on Martin Luther King's birthday. Last year in Central Park, Quincy Jones was master of ceremonies. A couple of years previous to that, Wynton Marsalis (whose jazz benefit concert was simultaneously going on at Avery Fisher Hall) crossed the Lincoln Center plaza with Itzhak Perlman to play Fiddlefest at Alice Tully Hall—and then the two of them went back and played the same gig at the other concert. Every single time, no matter where we are, the outpouring of love and appreciation almost blows us off the stage.

On February 13, 1996, I got an excited call from Wally Scheuer early in the morning. *Fiddlefest* had received an Academy Award nomination in the best documentary category. We were going to the Oscars!

The day before we were to fly to Los Angeles for the Oscar weekend, I was teaching at River East, and CNN was there, too, all day long—talking to the kids, filming us in class, and then interviewing me at my house immediately after school. They asked all kinds of serious questions, but at the end of the interview, they hit me with the big one: What was I going to wear to the Oscars?

"Well, I was invited to Donna Karan's studio to choose something from her collection," I said, laughing, "but the gowns all had these strategic cutouts—bare over here, slit up to there. I can't wear any of these; after all, I'm a schoolteacher. I have an image to maintain!" The crew laughed, too.

The next morning, I took a cab across town to Wally's office, and then we all went to the airport. He had told us we'd be flying first class, which I'd never done before. Nick and Lexi had given me firm instructions to take lots of pictures—they even wanted to see what first class looked like. Of course, when I got there, I couldn't bring myself to do that; I would've felt like an idiot!

Because we were nominees, we had been invited to wear jewelry from Harry Winston to the Oscar presentation. (Of course, we'd have to return it afterwards; too bad!) When the knock came on my hotel door, I opened it to see a very large, bruiser-type bodyguard and an elegant Asian woman with very long red finger-nails. She was carrying a big velvet envelope, which she opened with a dramatic flourish. There before me sparkled $800,000 worth of diamonds—a three-tiered diamond choker and earrings that looked like chandeliers in repose. In return for borrowing them, I had to sign a contract which made me liable for the jewels if I didn't return them before we left for the airport the next day. (In fact, the jewelry handlers came back for the goods promptly at 5:30 A.M.) I couldn't help but think how many violin teachers we could underwrite with just one earring. *Dear Mr. Winston: You don't know me, but . . .*

All over Hollywood, on Oscar afternoon, the routine for getting out of hotels and into the right limos (and from there to the Dorothy Chandler Pavilion and then out of the limos again) is more tightly choreographed than the Rockettes. They even go so far as to tell you precisely what time to leave your room and come down in the elevator. Once we were in the right line, I realized (courtesy of the enthusiastic fans just on the other side of the barrier) that Sharon Stone and her entourage were standing right ahead of us. Directly behind us was a group of people affiliated with *Babe*—we recognized them from the little stuffed pink pig each of them was carrying. Suddenly, I heard a woman quite near me say to her companion, "I don't know that one—do you know that one?" They were talking about me—clearly they'd been blinded by the diamonds! For the rest of the night, every ten minutes or so, I would abruptly fling my hands up to my ears to make sure the earrings were still there. The people sitting around me must've thought that something was seriously wrong.

The documentary film that won the Oscar that night was *Anne Frank Remembered*, an honorable "adversary" that we all respected greatly, especially given that it was the fiftieth anniversary of the publication of her diary. A few minutes before the winner of the category was announced, an incredible thing happened: An agreement was reached with Miramax that a feature film would be made based on my life and the documentary. The contract was signed right then and there.

After the ceremony was over, we slowly moved out of the auditorium, and a wave of people began melding from two directions into one. Pushed along by the swelling crowd, I glanced up and saw a tall, handsome man smiling and gesturing at me, an Oscar in each hand. "Bravo!" he was saying. It took me a couple of synapses before I realized it was Mel Gibson. "Who's he looking at?" I asked Susan.

"You!" she said, laughing. "He's congratulating you!" He had probably seen the documentary, she explained— almost everyone there that night had seen everything that had been nominated.

Wally, Susan, and Allan were invited to the Academy's Governor's Ball, and I went on ahead to the Miramax party to wait for them. When I got out of the limo, there was the proverbial red carpet. As I stepped out, someone handed me a glass of champagne. *This is not so bad*, I thought—and promptly stepped on Raquel Welch's foot.

A few minutes later, I was contentedly sampling all kinds of delicious hors d'oeuvres—shrimp and scallops, artichokes and asparagus, cheeses and caviar, and other things I didn't even know the names of, all of it stylishly presented by waiters sailing through the room, their serving trays held high above their heads. Suddenly, a very tall, black waiter swooped down to my level and offered me an hors d'oeuvre. "Thank you," I said. He bent down and whispered in my ear, "I think that what you do is worth more than what any of these people do."

I was startled. "How do you know what I do?" I asked.

He smiled. "I saw you on CNN this morning." As he walked away, he looked back over his shoulder and said, "And I loved what you said about the dress."

Other Voices: Nick and Alexi

Nick, 24, is a professional cellist and is studying for his Doctor of Musical Arts degree at SUNY at Stony Brook. Alexi, 22, recently graduated from Amherst College and has been accepted to Mt. Sinai Medical School in New York City.

Nick:

Everybody was worried when Mom moved us to East Harlem. Part of that was attributable to all the stereotypes about the ghetto, but there was also a concern about our being isolated—that the opportunities for Lexi and me would somehow be short-circuited. As it turned out, we got very good educations here, we both tracked into fine colleges and, I hope, challenging and respectable careers.

After I graduated from high school I went to New England Conservatory for a year and decided, *No, this is too narrow.* I thought I needed to get a real education.

So I enrolled in a dual degree program at Tufts University. There I was presented with a whole cafeteria of choices, and quickly figured out that that wasn't the place for me. I knew there was no way for me to do justice both to the work that a liberal arts degree requires and the focus and training required to be a musician. Most of all, I realized that if I wasn't prepared to give the music everything I had, I would end up a half-assed musician, and that was never an option for me. So I left Tufts, and focused completely on my music.

One of the reasons I started to play cello is because I hated working with Mom on the violin, just *hated* it. She has such a clear ear for intonation—even now, if I'm playing just the slightest bit out of tune, she flies off the handle, she can't take it for one minute.

I'm pursuing a doctorate in order to be able to teach at a very high level. I enjoy teaching kids the fundamentals, like Mom does, but I also enjoy the more cerebral aspect of musicianship, and that's where the degrees come in. I want to teach young artists who have already decided that they want to make a career of this, who understand the challenge of it, and what it costs— in a way, at the same stage of their careers that I am now. I'm very aware, and grateful, that she's given me the kind of music education she didn't have. Thanks to her encouragement and persistence, I've had the highest caliber of teacher. When I went to the Conservatory, it was to study with the top cello instructor, Lawrence Lesser. For cellists, Lesser is it; he's so esteemed that if he accepts you, you go. At Stonybrook, that person is Timothy Eddy. While there's no question Mom can open doors for me, I have to walk through them on my own. She may be able to get me an audition, but then I have to play.

With music, you don't see the results immediately. You go for weeks playing the same thing over and over. At some point, that doesn't feel creative, it feels like work. Then one day you're spinning out a phrase and suddenly discover how to play it more tenderly, make it more supple, and produce an entirely different sound. Making music really is like a journey—sometimes the road is tedious for long stretches, and other times it's astonishingly beautiful. The trick is just to hang in there and wait.

There are some people who want music to act upon them in a certain way—like a drink at the end of a hard day. But I can't be passive about what I hear. When I go to a concert, within minutes I'm dissecting things, analyzing every note, thinking, "That little nuance that cellist just put in, that was really beautiful, maybe I should try to do that." Before I know it, I'm working my way down a checklist. That's why, whenever I listen to the radio, it has to be something that has nothing to do with what I do every day. So I listen to NPR or talk radio.

When I was growing up in East Harlem, I listened to rap music. I wasn't into rock at all—I couldn't tell you anything the Police wrote, or anything that AC/DC did, because it wasn't something that was going on here.

Rap was. Some people really hate it, and some of it is pretty harsh, but it's a sound, a statement, an emotion, made by the young people who live here. The writers take idiomatic language and their own point of view to create something that's "inside." It's their street history, their "in" joke—it belongs to them. That's worth remembering, when people sneer.

In college, my roommates introduced me to jazz. I enjoyed the older stuff—for example, I love Duke Ellington. I never got into big band music; I really like the smaller versions of things. I listened to a lot of Chet Baker, a lot of Charles Mingus. Everyone said, oh, you have to get into Miles Davis—*Sketches in Spain* and *Certain Kind of Blue*. But I came to jazz by enjoying its beauty, not its progressiveness, and listening to Miles was like listening to science.

We were brought up with constant attention from Mom—in fact, I don't think we had a private minute. We were busy every hour of the day. On weekends we never slept over at other people's houses; instead, everyone came to our house. It didn't bother her if all of our friends were there—it meant she could keep a close eye on us.

When she first started talking about adopting Sophia, I didn't understand it. I guess I wanted her to be free of the responsibility of raising kids. Now that we were getting older, and I began to understand what we'd put her through, I wanted her to have a life. She's a beautiful, vibrant woman. But the bottom line is, she gets a lot of pleasure out of being a parent.

The fall after the baby came, Mom had a bad accident in the house. She was coming downstairs, the baby in her arms, when her sock got caught on the stair tread. Obviously she couldn't let go of Sophia to grab the railing. So she tried her best to shield the baby and went crashing down. She was lucky she didn't break her neck. As it was, her foot bent all the way back from the ankle, and the metatarsal just splintered. The amazing thing was that the baby never hit the ground—she never even cried.

All that winter, Mom had to sleep downstairs, in the kitchen, because she couldn't take the stairs—the cast wasn't the weight-bearing kind, and she was in a wheelchair. She took livery cabs everywhere—to school, with all the violins, in the snow and slush. At night, after teaching all day, she'd sit at the kitchen table, tired and in a lot of pain, and try to be the mother of two teenage boys and an infant. Lexi and I got called to full family duty—boy, did she ever issue the orders. It was change the baby, take the dog for a walk, do the dishes, do your homework, practice, practice. But we got through it.

She doesn't deal with Sophia the way she dealt with us. Part of that, of course, is because her own life has changed—she's not fighting for survival. But part of it relates to who my little sister is, what she's like. She was her own person from the time she was about six months old. Some kids are like that, even as babies— they've just got the program down. She's brilliant and strong, but not formed yet in terms of what's good, what has value and what doesn't. Some things are so attractive at that age; kids today have to be strong in different ways than we were.

From the time I was about six, I always thought Lexi needed protecting; I knew even when we were little that he had a tender heart. He didn't speak until he was about two, because I translated for him. My mother would say, "Nick, let him ask for the milk himself!"

When we got older, we fought all the time, physically—really punched and pushed each other around. I'd go to his desk and knock one thing off—a book, a pen—and then he'd walk over to my desk and knock one thing off. And then all hell would break loose. We set up a basketball court on the third floor of the house, and almost every game ended in a two-man brawl. Lexi was a terrific athlete—he had huge hands, even as a kid, which is why he's so gifted on the piano.

Now we're adults, both struggling with our personal lives, trying to figure out women and relationships. We saw Mom hurt, we saw her go through the hard times. How do you decide to take the risks? How do you decide who's worth your trust? How do you not hurt other people, or get hurt yourself? It's hard to see it clearly sometimes, through my memories of what Mom went through.

No matter what we do, though, I know she wants us to live close to her. I think she hopes that if everything goes right, she'll be able to see in her own kitchen, or in the garden out back, the same picture she saw when she was growing up—the grandparents and the parents, the aunts and uncles, fifteen people around the table at any given meal.

There are two distinct parts of my mother: One is the musician, the artist, with the truly creative soul; the other part is the teacher. Increasingly, she sees herself identified as a teacher, being asked to come and tell other people how to do what she does. She would rather that they come and watch her. You can't standardize her energy, her motivation and determination, her unshakable belief that every child can learn to play the violin. But you can watch how she takes the kids through the steps, and you can see the results. She's got a formula, a technique, that's all her own, tailored to her personality and to the needs of her students. Just as her teaching technique grew out of watching other people, other teachers could do the same by watching her, and then adapting their own technique to what their students need.

This woman has the worst memory of anyone I know, yet she remembers the names of all the kids she's taught, their brothers and their sisters, what was going on with their parents, how they were doing with school, what they played in a recital. She can't remember her phone number half the time—she can't remember *my* phone number—but she doesn't forget the kids. If there's a choice between having fame or knowing she would be able to continue to teach, she'll take the teaching every time.

Mom would be the first to argue that she's not out to produce virtuosos. She just wants to give them a way into the arts, into creativity, into a different way of looking at their own possibilities. Yes, she makes them work hard; once in a while, somebody has trouble with the work ethic and drops out. But she won't coddle anyone—it wouldn't be fair to the ones who hang in there even when they're struggling.

Last winter the *New York Times* and *People* magazine reported the story of a Chinese music teacher here in the city. He and his wife cashed in their savings, they bought a lot of instruments, and now they're teaching violin in a Queens elementary school—for free. And everyone says, "Isn't that wonderful!" No, it's not! The couple is wonderful, yes, what they're giving is a great gift. But the situation stinks. For one thing, they're teaching the kids during the school lunch break—so clearly, there's no time allotted by the system, and there's no money coming from the system. So the system, in essence, gets a free ride. If that's such a terrific deal, why don't we ask teachers to volunteer their time? Why don't we ask school bus drivers and custodians to volunteer their time?

No, this isn't a good story, it's a bad story, and its biggest flaw is that it makes everybody feel comfortable. Legislators who cut arts budgets shouldn't be bragging about that; they should be pilloried for not having any foresight. They're not advocates for children.

Alexi:

I was always acutely aware that I was a white kid in a predominantly black and Latino community. That was really apparent on the basketball court at Jefferson Park, near our house. You definitely had to prove yourself there. For a long time, nobody would pick us to be on a team, but after we proved we could play, kids began to look beyond our color.

I was completely in love with basketball. I'd dribble the ball all the way to the store, all the way to school. I'd be playing at the park, under the lights, and completely lose track of time. Then all of a sudden here comes Mom, with the dog, and she'd do everything but put the leash on me, hauling me back home and giving me hell all the way. When I think of the guys I knew who didn't make the right choices, I figure they just didn't have a mom who wasn't afraid to drag them home from the basketball court.

Once I was on my way to play ball in the park—I was in the seventh grade, I think—and I went past, or maybe even through, a group of kids from another school. They jumped me; one kid smacked me on the back of the head, they took away the basketball, hollered some things. Talked trash. After I got home and got myself cleaned up, I told some of my neighborhood friends what had happened. We went right out, tracked the other guys down, and retrieved the basketball. The kids who jumped me and took the ball were black and Hispanic; the kids who backed me up were also black and Hispanic. Race was always a factor, of course, but mostly, our loyalties and affiliations were about neighborhood.

You can't argue with my mother when she's made a decision. When she gets into a Roberta mindset, don't even try to change her mind. She's so emotional—there's no filter on what she's feeling. It's like you can see her heart. Half the planet is in therapy trying to get access to their emotions, and here's Mom, with total access to hers all the time. It must be like getting too much radio reception.

When Nick was eleven or twelve, she bought him a great dirt bike. She spent about four hundred dollars on it—big money for us at the time. One afternoon he was playing basketball at Jefferson Park with some of the neighborhood kids and one of the bigger guys, about sixteen, asked if he could ride the bike. Our friend Louie knew this guy, and he warned us, "No, no, don't let him do it." But Nick figured what the heck. So off goes the big guy and off goes Nick's bike.

An hour, maybe more, goes by, we're waiting at the park and still no bike. When we finally went home and told Mom, she went right over the top. "Where does that kid live?" she hollered. It turned out that Louie knew where—in the projects, which at that point were so scary that even the city ambulance guys wouldn't respond to 911 calls. But that didn't slow Mom down— she jumped into the car, with us and Louie, and we drove around in the dark from building to building, looking for the right one. When Louie pointed it out, Mom went sprinting into the building. "Don't take the stairs!" Louie yelled, but she headed for the stairwell, which ranked right up there in terms of being dangerous. Identifying herself as a teacher, she talked to the guy's grandmother, who of course said that she hadn't seen either him or the bike. "I don't want to get the police in on this," Mom said. "But I want that bike back." An hour or so later, the bike mysteriously showed up in front of our house. It was dinged up, but it was there. To this day, I'm still not sure if what she did that night was about the money, or her sons, or her outrage at somebody trying to screw us, or a combination of all three. We were pretty blown away at how audacious— or stupid, or brave—it was.

Money never played a large role in our lives, and it doesn't now in terms of the decisions Nick and I make. We learned early on that money doesn't buy happiness— which was a good thing, since we never had much of it. In fact, the people we know who have money don't seem, in many ways, to be all that much better off than we are. What we always did have is Mom's sense of quality: what a quality instrument is, what a quality person is. Aesthetics, the way everything looks, or should look, that's very important to her. There's nothing in the house that's not her design. She believes that the way things are set up, from the flowers in a vase to the food on a plate or the way her violin kids stand before they begin to play, adds to the quality of life, the quality of a performance.

Whatever you do, you're supposed to give it everything you've got. It was so hard to study music with her; she expected so much from all her students, and twice as much from us. If you brought home a 90 on a test, she asked, "Why not one hundred?"

When we moved into the house, she put in a Radio Shack intercom on all three floors, so she could keep track of where we were and what we were doing without hollering or running up and down the stairs. After school, I'd be practicing piano downstairs, Nick would be upstairs playing the cello. Since I was down where Mom usually was, where there was no television or anything like that, I could never slack off. Nick, however, was safely out of range. He taped himself playing cello and he'd put the tape on so she could hear it downstairs on the intercom. Then he'd watch TV or read. She didn't catch on to that for a long time!

On my own projects—my films, the papers I wrote for school, playing the piano—I really labor. I don't do things haphazardly. Nick's a perfectionist, too, especially about the cello, his teaching, anything having to do with his music. Of all of us, I definitely have the most tolerance for disorder—my process is a little messier than Mom's, Nick's, or Sophia's. I come to things in a different way. (And later, usually!)

I learned to appreciate Mom's teaching style while studying piano with Mitsuko Ichimura. Ms. Ichimura had a very precise way of teaching—very strict and demanding. I was scared shitless of her, in fact. The interesting thing about strictness is that it has consistency—you always know what's expected. You know you have to come prepared or pay the consequences. I think there always has to be a little of that— a little anxiety, a little edge—to push you into being better. And the student has to want to please the teacher. For one thing, if she's happy, she won't be so critical (which is pretty important to a little kid)! For another, it's a kick to rise to someone's expectation of you.

There has to be a balance between strictness and passion. Because that's frequently where the flaw is— no passion. The kids don't see it, the teachers don't have it. Or if they do, maybe it gets squashed out of them pretty quickly. I was lucky—I had passionate teachers.

Nick and I have certain basic core values that Mom instilled in us that form the way we make decisions. My interest in being a doctor is mostly because she told us over and over that no matter what we did in life, no matter how much money we had, if we weren't passionate about what we were doing, and doing something beneficial to others, we weren't going to be happy. Ever since my junior year in high school, in Bronx Science, I wanted to go into medicine—it seemed the perfect balance between working with people, and doing science, which I loved.

My brother is a natural leader; everybody always looked up to him. I don't know how early I decided that he was my role model, but it always seemed the most natural thing in the world. After he went off to college, Mom and I would watch *Little House on the Prairie* and cry during the sad parts—we had been a team for so long, it was hard to start going off in separate directions.

No matter how old we get, we're still Roberta's kids. It's hard to think of ourselves in any other way; certainly, Mom still thinks of us like that. For instance, I've been talking for months about my plan to go to Chile before med school, but she's completely convinced that something awful will happen to me there. This is a woman who moved to 118th Street and started tearing down walls and fighting with subcontractors who were really street guys—and then tells her grownup sons that she wants us to be cautious! She forgets that we saw her go into that building after that bicycle.

In a way, being part of her decision to adopt Sophia forced Nick and me to become more adult. I still have such a vivid picture of the baby, sitting in her infant seat, on the floor in front of the piano. I was so struck by her vulnerability and beauty. Here was this tiny girl, our little sister, who needed us. And then I realized we needed her just as much.

I spent a summer in El Salvador after my sophomore year in college because I wanted to find out more about the people my sister comes from, to understand more about her roots. I taught English and lived with a Salvadoran family, a single mother with two kids. I felt so connected to the woman because she reminded me so much of Mom. The effects of the war in El Salvador were so devastating, and still so evident, that even the simplest tasks and comforts took on enormous proportions. However, despite the hardships, the family found ways to be happy. It put any hardship I've ever endured or might endure into significant perspective.

Sophia is growing up with a bicultural identity—being in this neighborhood and going to school at River East is a vital part of that process for her. She will be a strong Latin woman at a time when this country is finally beginning to realize that's a very cool thing to be. Finding her own way to do art will be important for her. She's so musical, and she wants to dance; she recently auditioned for the School of American Ballet, which puts on *The Nutcracker* each year at Lincoln Center. She could probably become a painter, she has the same kind of eye Mom has.

Nick and I get on Mom sometimes because she's not anywhere near as strict with Sophia as she was with us. Of course, Sophia herself has an amazing steel will. She's definitely a survivor, but she's also soft, and creative, and delicate. She's really a reflection of my mother in that way. I've never really thought about this until now, but maybe they're more alike, more destined to be mother and daughter, than anybody really knows.

The Garden that Grew in a Different Place

"One way we grapple with ideas is through the arts. To cut kids off from an essential part of their nature is fundamentally wrong. If schools are here to enhance our human qualities, a school that has ignored the artist in us has done damage."
—DEBORAH MEIER

When I was girl, dreaming about what my own life would be, I never could have imagined it would come to this: an unprecedented concert in Carnegie Hall, an Oscar-nominated documentary, a feature film with Meryl Streep playing me, and now this book, where I'm trying to figure out how I got here. And then there are three great kids, Opus 118, and 175 eager violin students this year alone. How *did* I get here?

The answer is, I was supposed to be here. My life, and everything in it, is a garden that grew in a different place. John Lennon didn't set out to be a philosopher; nevertheless, he was the one who observed that "life is what happens when you're making other plans."

Shortly after the school shootings in Littleton, Colorado, a television reporter was talking to Sissela Bok, the author and philosopher whose most recent book is *Mayhem: Violence as Public Entertainment* (Addison-Wesley). When asked what kinds of indicators point to the kids most likely to commit violent crime, Bok responded that in her opinion, the red flags are not poverty versus wealth, or urban versus rural, or black versus white. Rather, she said, the kids to worry about were the "emotionally underprivileged."

We're not, as a society, doing much about helping kids create an inner self, an inner life. We take care of so many other things—nutrition, dental health, vaccinations, look both ways, don't talk to strangers, don't smoke, don't use drugs. It's as if we're constructing a building that has a good roof and attractive exterior walls, but no structure inside to hold it up. Maybe we think the spiritual part will take care of itself, that it will somehow develop organically—when in fact it's the very thing we need to put first.

Recently, I attended a Petra Foundation awards ceremony in Washington, D.C., in which the new fellows of the foundation were honored. In the eight years since my introduction to Petra, I've come to know and respect the men and women in its network: true heroes, as its literature states, "taking personal risks as they contribute to human freedom." They advocate for minorities, for prisoners, for the poor and migrant workers; they work to eradicate land mines and homelessness and hate groups—these people are literally saving lives. How, I've wondered, do I fit in?

Al Kirkland was recognized by Petra in 1994 for developing a number of after-school programs for kids in the New York City neighborhood of Washington Heights; currently he's in the process of creating a new after-school center sponsored by the Police Athletic League (PAL). This year, he brought PAL kids with him to the Petra conference; some of them spoke about how they were overcoming great obstacles and transforming not only their lives, but the lives of younger kids for whom they'd become role models. When one young man, eighteen or nineteen, was asked by a foundation fellow, "What do kids need from us? How can we help you turn it around?" he had only one answer, which he repeated over and over again. "You know what you've gotta do? You've gotta *make* us believe we can do it," he pleaded. "Make us *believe* we can do it! Make us believe *we can do it*."

That's how I fit in. My work saves lives, too.

Since we're all trying to figure out what we've lost as a society over the years, and what we can do to restore ourselves and our children and our communities, I'd like to puts arts education—music, dance, drama, painting—on the list of things to consider. As Arnold Steinhardt said after the Carnegie Hall concert, "It was about handing down cultural values, human values— the fiddle was only a medium!"

Kids have emotions, strong emotions. They have

creativity and humor; they get frustrated, and their hearts break. They feel anger and fear and sorrow and, yes, hatred. They have dreams and ideas. We owe it to them, and to ourselves, to give them a place, a way, to channel what they feel, because that emotion is like molten lava. If it doesn't find a place to go, if it cannot find expression, it will simply burst up through the ground, tearing the earth, destroying everything in its path.

Our brains have to process so much at once. We are bombarded with information and sound—movies, video games, televisons: In many homes, the TV is on all the time. Add to this the ambient sounds of other people's music, shouting, car horns. We're all on the receiving end of the stimulation, and children are especially vulnerable. They haven't yet learned how to defend themselves against it.

Just as music (both playing and listening) can have a positive effect on a child's brain, stress, abuse, and trauma will push the process in the opposite direction. Some studies show that in kids with a history of abuse, certain areas of the brain are as much as 30 percent smaller than would normally be expected. With repeated stress, the brain tries to reorganize itself. The result is chaos, causing everything from hyperactivity and attention deficit disorder to self-control problems.

One of my students often runs out of the music room when I start making demands, even the most gentle ones: how to hold a bow, how to stand straight. When she first came to class, after three years of special ed, she was being mainstreamed into a "regular" class-room experience—a new setting for her. She didn't know how to pay attention to me, she couldn't under-stand even the simplest instructions—she simply re-ceived information in a different way. And when she got it wrong, it made her angry. It took a long time to teach her to think about the way she picked up the violin, picked up the bow, the way she was standing—and still, she'll sometimes run and hide when it gets hard. But she always comes back and she always tries again. Be-cause she *believes* she can do it, she *likes* doing it—and she's getting very good.

In Deborah Meier's book, she quotes the eminent social historian Henry Louis Gates, Jr.: "Any human being suf-ficiently motivated can fully possess another culture, no matter how 'alien' it may appear to be. But there is no tolerance without respect—and no respect without knowledge." That's an underlying tenet of the school where I've been teaching—where I learned to teach, re-ally—for almost twenty years.

In addition to Catholic, Jewish, and traditional Christian kids, CPE and River East schools enroll Seventh-Day Adventists, Jehovah's Witnesses, Black Muslims, and fundamentalist Christians, whose parents have chosen the school because of its reputation for fairness and tolerance. There are no entrance exams or qualifying tests; admission is offered by lottery selection. Because of the critical importance of family synergy, we also take all siblings. Over the years, the staff gets to know the families well, and vice versa. We're all invested in each other: We're a community. When there are hardships, nobody walks away; when there are victories, they belong to everyone.

There are always many more applicants for the violin program than we can take, so, like CPE, we use a lottery system, too. Very often, a child whose family belongs to a particular religious group isn't allowed to play anything patriotic, or anything reflecting a specific religious ideology. In fact, cultural diversity raises all kinds of interesting questions for these kids. There are an increasing number of scholarships and grants for minority kids that white kids can't apply for—the MAP (Musical Advancement Program) at Juilliard, for instance. I always explain that if I were a student in this classroom now, I wouldn't be allowed to apply for MAP, because I'm not from a Latino or Spanish background, or African-American. Someone gave a grant to Juilliard because they wanted to open the doors of classical music to more people of color. Some of my violin kids are walking through those doors.

Here are some intriguing facts and figures that I've been accumulating in the past year, ranging from newspaper clippings, statistics hurriedly written down on restaurant napkins, and stories from publications such as

Newsweek, U.S. News & World Report, Parents maga-zine, *Family Circle* magazine, and the *American School Board Journal*:

- More than four million students are coming into the public school system every year; there's a baby boom happening right now that will dwarf the post–World War II boom I grew up in.

- Some studies show that kids learn 50,000 words in their first four years.

- More than half of the money that supports music in public schools comes from fund-raising, not taxes. That includes everything from bake sales to philan-thropy.

- In Japan, every child, from grades one through nine, takes two hours of music instruction a week. Class-rooms are equipped with a piano and desktop key-boards for each student. This is in addition to after-school activities such as chorus, band, and or-chestra.

- In Germany, from kindergarten through twelfth grade, students get a minimum of two forty-five-minute music classes per week. In those countries, the school year averages 240 days a year, compared with 180 days for American kids. By the time German kids graduate, they've logged 33 percent more years of education than American students.

- In the Third International Mathematics and Science Study in 1995, United States eighth graders placed twenty-seventh out of forty nations (reported by Achieve, in Cambridge, Massachusetts).

- In the SAT exams, students who have taken music or instrument instruction scored on average fifty-one points higher on the verbal and thirty-nine points higher on the math portion than kids who didn't (The College Board: Profiles of SAT and Achievement Test Takers, 1995).

- According to professors Frances Rauscher and Gordon Shaw of the University of California at Irvine, only ten minutes of listening to Mozart's Piano Sonata K448 significantly increased the spatial relationship scores of college students on IQ tests. They dubbed this result (first reported in 1993) the "Mozart" effect.

- In 1996, a team of researchers led by Drs. Shaw and Rauscher studied seventy-eight children, three to four years old, divided into three groups. Thirty-four received private piano keyboard lessons; twenty received equally frequent private computer lessons; twenty-four served as controls for the study, receiving either singing lessons or no special lessons at all. Of all the kids, only the ones who took piano lessons showed a "significant improvement"—34 percent— on spatial-temporal tests (spatial and temporal reasoning are key for math and science). In a similar study of three-year-olds, those who took piano and singing lessons for six months scored 80 percent higher than those who did not.

- Georgia hospitals send Mozart cassettes home with every newborn; Florida is mandating state-funded daycare centers and preschools to play classical music for at least one half hour per day.
- A recent collaboration between the National Academy of Recording Arts and Sciences Foundation and Enfamil, the baby-formula company, has produced a classical CD entitled *Smart Symphonies*, distributed free to many hospitals and sent home with new mothers.

There is no substitute for a teacher. I believe absolutely in the power of teachers—the ones I had, the ones my children have had, the ones I see around me every day, changing children's lives. Most adults who have achieved any measure of success (and I'm not limiting this to economic success, but expanding it to personal, creative, spiritual, and emotional) can usually give you the name of at least one teacher who said or did something that excited and inspired them.

All over the country, philanthropic organizations are devoting countless hours and millions of dollars to providing arts education in the schools. The solution, they think, is a complex and beautiful patchwork of outreach programs that send artists into the schools and bring kids to museums, theaters, and concert halls. Two for the price of one: The artists are supported, the kids get art. On the surface, it's hard to argue with the effectiveness and even the generosity of this idea.

But for kids, short-term exposures aren't the only answer: We've got it backwards. A visiting artist leaves, a museum trip comes to an end—and the result is the kids have been teased by a dream that seems far, far out of their reach. What must come first is the presence of the hands-on art teacher (that's me) to provide the bridge, the consistency, the connection between each child and that artist—and to *make* the child believe, "I can do it!" A kid has to hold an instrument, a violin or a paintbrush, get clay under his fingernails, make mistakes, get things dirty. Kids need to *do* it.

When commentators, politicians, and social scientists all talk about people working together, especially in an urban environment, more often than not they use the sports metaphor: This is a team effort. But in sports, each time someone wins, someone else loses. I believe that the metaphor of an orchestra is much better: many different individuals and instruments and sounds, creating one effort, one unified moment—something beautiful. Orchestra members play as one, yet they have to be aware of each other as individual players. They make both one sound and a combination of sounds. It's winning together.

Our children deserve to study music and the arts. It's time for us, as a society, to face what we've lost in our schools and what it has cost us. We must—we *must*—bring the arts back as a fundamental part of the curriculum. Creating art is both physical and spiritual—when my students play music, they're transformed, transcendent, lost in the moment, but also completely grounded in the doing of it. Music has such power—to move someone, to change someone. Creativity has its very roots in nature; rhythm itself begins with the beat of the human heart.

Other Voices: America's Story

*J*ose Miguel Rojas *won a lottery position* in my beginner's class the year he turned five. How his first year of violin lessons progressed formed one of the underlying themes of the *Fiddlefest/Small Wonders* documentary. However, many other things happened to Jose and his family during that time, and much has happened in the years since.

America, Jose's mother, has large brown eyes and a lovely, high-cheekboned face, somber in repose but lit from within when she talks about her children. Jose, small for his age (he's now twelve, and in junior high), has eyes like his mother's, an indomitable spirit, and a wealth of opinions. He is the protective big brother to two younger sisters, Anastasia and Destiny, and all three are enthusiastic musicians-in-progress—maybe, someday, a chamber music trio.

JOSE: When I was about four, I was walking in Central Park one day with my mom. I saw someone playing music on something under his chin. He played it with a stick in his hand. My mother told me it was a violin.

AMERICA: "I like the way it sounds," he said. "I would like to know how to do that." I just shook my head. We had been through so much with this little boy, I didn't believe such a thing could ever happen.

I was born and raised here in New York, but all my family had come from Puerto Rico. When Jose was born, I was already forty. With my first husband I had four kids—Debbie was twenty; Benjamin, fifteen; Nicholas, thirteen; and Josh, twelve. My second husband, Jose Senior, was from Santo Domingo, the Dominican Republic. Jose Miguel was his first child.

When I was at the end of my pregnancy with him, my water broke. I went right away to the hospital, but the doctors said I wasn't dilated enough to stay there—they told me to go home. I did, but I wasn't happy about it. A mother knows when her baby is coming.

After that, I was in hard labor for ten, maybe twelve more hours—by the time we went back to the hospital and Jose was born, I was pretty beat up and he had suffered oxygen deprivation. It was a very rough beginning for him.

By Jose's first birthday, I knew he was having trouble. For one thing, he didn't ever try to talk. Of course, he had his big brothers and sister to do his talking for him, but still, this baby hardly made a sound. And then after he had his anti-meningitis shots, he got terribly sick, with a very high fever and seizures. We rushed him to the hospital and sure enough, it was a viral infection. They had to drain the swelling from his brain and give him intravenous antibiotics.

After that, I was pretty sure he was partly deaf, although none of the doctors wanted to admit it. But I knew. Jose wasn't like my other ones. He was so quiet, like he was living in a silent world of his own. When he tried to communicate with us, it was such a struggle for him, and he'd get frustrated, and then just weep. Pretty soon it was like he was sad all the time.

When he started to walk, Jose was always up on tip-toes, like babies are in the beginning. But this little one, he never got *down* off his toes. The muscles in his legs were pulled up too tight, like thick, knotted rubber bands—he could not get his heels down on the floor. I saw also that his fingers were curling in on his palms, like little claws. He couldn't open his hands all the way, and he couldn't close his fingers tight enough to hold things.

The doctors decided that the diagnosis for all of this was cerebral palsy. He wouldn't ever be able to speak right, they said. He probably wouldn't ever learn to read or write, or be able to walk without limping or being off balance. And he would have great difficulty with touch—the sensation of touching something with his hands would always be painful for him.

Jose's grandfather was blind, and listened to the radio all the time. One day he heard about a special place—the "eye and ear," he called it. "You have to take the baby there," he insisted when he gave me all the details. "America, you have to do something."

Lucky for me, the specialist who did the tests on Jose just fell in love with him. "We will find a school for him," she promised.

At nineteen months, Jose went off to the East Village School for Special Education, down on 14th Street. Every day, a little yellow bus came to get him. Watching that bus go down the street is when I began to believe that things might change, and they did. First, he got braces for his legs, to strengthen the muscles and bring him down off his toes. And slowly, he began to talk. Well, actually, he began to sing. That's how the school said to teach him. "Singing will help him learn," they said. Repeating verses over and over would help him know the connection between what he's thinking in his brain and what comes out of his mouth.

My husband didn't speak English until then. He had to learn it to teach Jose to sing. Every night we walked around in circles, my husband, the other kids, and me, like a small parade, from the living room through the kitchen and back around the other side, singing, "The wheel on the bus goes 'round and 'round," over and over. By the time that little boy was four, he was making progress, although he sang everything. Even when he asked for a peanut butter sandwich, he sang the question.

At first, Jose hated his braces—he was so little, and to support the heavy braces he had to wear shoes two sizes bigger than his actual size. We learned how to do exercises on Jose's feet, pushing, pulling, flexing them, so he could feel what it was to stretch. We tried to be gentle, but it was hard for him. He cried, we cried. He was still such a little boy.

My husband was having a bad time, being very sad for his little son and yet also embarrassed. This was a proud Latin man, the first one in his generation to have a child. His family, his mother, his sisters and brothers—he felt like they were making judgments on him because of all the things that were wrong with his son. Our daughter Anastasia was born when Jose was about a year old—she was beautiful and her daddy welcomed her with great joy, but it didn't take away his sadness about Jose.

JOSE: My papa's culture said boys play baseball, boys learn to box, boys are athletic. That's what real boys do. Felipe and Matty Alou came from his country, and Juan Marichal—and now, Sammy Sosa. I always knew their names. Papa had dreams for me before I was even born, and now here I was, with problems. He wanted me to play sports, to run around, to have energy. So I would go to Central Park with him, and we would play together. We would take turns batting and pitching the baseball, and I would try to run and kick the soccer ball. And I didn't do so bad.

AMERICA: When it was time for Jose to "graduate" from East Village School, they said it was time to find a special ed program for him. *Here we go,* I thought, with a bad feeling in my stomach. One of my older kids went through public school special ed, and it was a disaster. These little ones come out of a small program, where they've had help and attention, and they feel pretty brave, pretty smart. Then they hit public school and the whole thing falls apart. They have a label on them, "special ed," which to the kids means "dummy."

So now school is a horrible place where you suffer because you're different. You decide you hate the kids, you hate the teachers, and you hate learning. And you quit school, which my older son did. And he never went back. From that, there has been a lot of heartbreak.

Just because a kid is different doesn't mean he needs some special "program." OK, maybe a little something extra—but maybe not, because who really knows when a kid is that young what might happen in just another week or two? Ask any mom of three kids—did they all start tying their shoes at the same time? No.

My husband and I didn't have much, but we weren't poverty cases. We were working, the kids were eating, everybody had clothes. The bills got paid, most of them. But there was nothing extra. So private school for Jose, even Catholic school, was not possible. We had to go with what there was in public school, but even that . . . well, if you just accept what they give you, you don't get much—you have to fight. So I fought.

I called a man named John Falco, the deputy superintendent of our district. "They assigned my kid to a school named River East," I said. "They're going to stick him with the special ed label. I can't allow this. I'm not risking this one, he's come too far. Please, you have to help." Falco knew exactly what I was talking about. He didn't talk down, he didn't treat me like I was a raving crazy. He explained how River East was part of the Central Park East School, how it was "alternative," and how the teachers treated each kid with respect. There were all kinds of kids there, he said—poor, middle-class, all colors, even some "specials"—but nobody made a big deal over it.

So off we went to check out River East. For hours, we walked everywhere in that school. It was bright and clean, like they had pride in it. We looked in the classrooms, we met some people—teachers, students. The whole time little Jose is clomping up and down three flights of stairs with his braces, but nobody gives us a funny look or makes a big fuss. It was just, Hello, how are you, nice to meet you. I liked the way it felt.

JOSE: The first time I saw Roberta and her violin, it was my first year at River East, in pre-K. There was a potluck dinner at school. All the families go, and every class does a skit. I was a pirate, with an eye patch. When it came time for the violin kids, they came out and played *We Shall Overcome*. It was the first song I had ever heard on the violin. The music just came into my head.

AMERICA: When Roberta's group started to play *Overcome*,
Jose was like a statue. Before that, he was
wiggling around, all excited because of his skit
and the pirate thing—but when that song started,
he quit moving like somebody hit his off button.
When the song was over, he said, "I want to play
like that lady." And I thought to myself, *Yeah,
right*. This kid wears braces, he can barely hear
or speak—now he wants to play the violin? This
is a boy who, at this point in his life, has to sing
in order to ask for a peanut butter sandwich!

JOSE: I couldn't not look at Roberta, and it was like she
was looking right back at me, bowing and
smiling. Her face when she plays is really pretty.
And those kids were making the most beautiful
sound. When the end-of-the-year concert came,
we went to that one, too. I was feeling the music,
I just knew I had to do it. So I asked my mom to
let me put my name in the lottery.

When I got the letter that said I was accepted, I
couldn't believe it happened. I was so happy! Then some
of the older kids told me, "Oh, no, Jose, you don't want
go to violin classes with Roberta. You better think about
this again, because we're warning you, this lady is really
rough." And I started to get a little scared.

The very first day, it was kind of nervous for me.
But I tried to be calm, because inside, I knew I had
something I wanted. But I got scared anyway, especially
when Roberta picked me to go up front so she could

demonstrate on me. She helps you hold the violin—well, really, she holds it, but she puts your fingers where they will go someday when you know what you're doing. And she does the bow, she plays *Twinkle, Twinkle,* and it's like you're playing it. "Relax, Jose, and pretend you're a little puppet," she said. "I'll do the work, you be a soft puppet." And it worked—I made that sound!

AMERICA: But your hands . . .

JOSE: Oh, yeah. My hands didn't work right, my fingers were still curling in. I had to learn to concentrate with my brain on making the muscles and tendons work. I'd stand there for a long time and my feet would get really tired. Sometimes I still had my leg braces on, but sometimes I didn't. When my fingers curled up, I would push too hard on the strings and hold the bow too tight. And Roberta would help me be loose. She showed me how to hold a ball in my hand and work my fingers—on, off, on, one finger at a time, ten times each. Pretty soon I learned to grab on. Now, the violin fits in my hand just right.

The first three weeks of lessons, Roberta was kind of nice and patient. But after we got our own violins and started playing, whew, she used to really scold us. "Stop plucking!" "Pay attention!" "This is important!" Those kids who warned me were right—she was really tough. And I learned, Jose, you better practice!

AMERICA: It's funny to remember now, but he wasn't even six yet, and he was so serious about that violin. He would come home after school with a little-old-man face and practice and practice. *Screech, screech, screech.* Oh, it hurt my head just to listen to him. His big brothers and his sister would say, "Ma, make him stop! He's killing us!" And his daddy was not happy about this violin stuff.

JOSE: My papa, I couldn't get him to listen to me, not even for five minutes. I'd say, "Papa, could you please hear me a little bit?" And he'd kind of make a face, and say, "OK, maybe later," and then watch TV or whatever. I would walk away, feeling like I was about to cry, but I didn't want him to see me. I would go in my room and stick my music up on the wall with tape, and practice so I would be good for Roberta the next day.

AMERICA: During Jose's first year in violin, the film people—Wally Scheuer and Allan Miller and Susan Kaplan—were around school almost all the time, working on the *Fiddlefest* documentary. At first, the kids were all jumpy about that, but pretty soon it wore off and they almost forgot the cameras were there. When I look now at the scene where Jose actually wins the lottery and comes running out to the playground to tell me and my husband this happy news, it breaks my heart. This little kid, his eyes all shining, and this man who loves him so much, but just doesn't get what it is with Roberta and this violin thing.

When they put out the notices for the big Carnegie Hall concert, with all Roberta's kids playing with the famous violinists—Perlman and Stern and the rest—Jose was still too new, so he didn't play in it. But I got tickets anyway. I talked my husband into going, but he wasn't happy about it. We took the subway down to 57th Street and on the way we had a huge fight. "This violin thing is not part of me," he said. "This is not my way."

"It might not be your way," I said to him, "but it's Jose's way now. Our son is going to be strong in a different way." I told him we were going into Carnegie Hall, and if he didn't want to go with us, well, that was up to him. But I was going. He came in with us, but for the whole concert he was grumpy and restless in his seat.

JOSE: On the subway, my father was really yelling in Spanish, "*No, no, no,* no son of mine!" Even with my bad hearing, I knew what he was saying. Then came my mother's answer. "Even if you do not respect Jose's ways, I will respect them, and I will support him." I was sad about Papa, but what my mother said gave me a strong feeling. And being in Carnegie Hall, where we had never been, to hear that music in such a place, to see my teacher on the stage—it was like a dream.

AMERICA: In Roberta's program, there's Latino kids, Asian kids, island black kids, African black kids, middle-class white kids from across town, and each one carries the parents' culture with them. Maybe the mom and the dad accept and support violin, maybe sometimes they don't. Learning to play an instrument is hard enough for a child, but when somebody at home is mad about the learning . . . well, it was hard for us. But I had to make that fight.

The sorrow is, there was so much I did wrong with my older kids, and they paid the price for that—in what they didn't learn, in what they did wrong, in how they hurt themselves in stupid or sad ways. It broke my heart, to look back and see where things could have been different. I decided it would be different for Jose and Anastasia, and the music gave us a direction to go.

After one year, when it came time for the end-of-the-year concert at school, this time Jose was going to play. I asked—even begged—my husband, please, please, come to this one. And we invited his side of the family to the big rehearsal the day before. Everyone made excuses to say no. It was very hurtful. But my husband agreed, yes, OK, he will come, at least to the rehearsal.

He sat in the seat in front of me, I'm right behind. We talked a little, waiting for the beginning. When the music started, he faced front and sat straight up—this time, he promised, he would pay good attention.

When Jose really started to play, I saw that my husband's body was shaking. His shoulders and back—I thought, is he crying or something? I leaned forward.

"What's wrong?" I whispered. He shook his head, but would not turn around. "Nothing," he whispered back.

When we got home, my husband was very quiet for a while. "I never, never thought he could do something like this," he said finally. "I didn't understand it. I didn't understand him." And then he said to his son, "Jose, if this is what you want, I am your father and I will support you. I will respect you and cheer you."

Maybe he had been afraid in the beginning, because of all of the strikes against Jose, that his boy was going to try to do something and fail. And get hurt. But now that fear was over.

The next day, at the real concert, we all went to the auditorium together, the big kids, too, and what a good time we had. You cry every single time the kids play *We Shall Overcome*, you can't help it. And then the parents all stand and cheer. My big kids just shook their heads in amazement at Jose. "We can't believe he did this," they said.

JOSE: When we came out after the concert, Papa was laughing. "We are going to have a celebration!" There was a bodega near a park, and he went into it and brought out a six-pack of beer and two cans of soda. Then we all sat down on the stone wall. "We're having a celebration," Papa said to everyone who walked by us. "This was my son's concert day, and I'm celebrating it!"

AMERICA: I used to get home from the hospital at about three, three-thirty, in the afternoon, and make a big pot of strong coffee. My husband's mother wasn't doing so good, so after he would get back from work—he was a carpenter—he would go down to her apartment for a few hours and spend some time there, maybe watch TV or read the paper with her. After a while, he'd come up, we would have our coffee together, black with a lot of sugar, and then he would go back downstairs.

One afternoon, I came home and made the coffee as usual. Jose and Annie were home from school, they're doing their music and their homework. It was noisy, busy—with little kids, you lose track of time, you know? They were talking about how they wanted to watch a movie on TV, a Bible story, Cain and Abel. So I made dinner and they turned on the movie—and I was thinking, wait a minute here, it's pretty late, where is my husband? I started watching the clock.

Then my husband's brother calls from his mother's apartment. "You better come down here," he says, "because your husband is not feeling good." When I get into the apartment, my husband is standing, kind of shaky, by a chair. Something is wrong with his face, his color isn't right. In an odd voice, he says, "America, I am getting a stroke."

That can't be true, I think. Yes, he has high blood pressure, but he's controlling it with medication. And besides, he's only in his mid-forties.

"My arm is numb, and my leg," says my husband, but now he's looking behind me, over my shoulder. And he says, "No matter what happens, you watch out for the kids, watch out for your mother." I turn and look behind me, and there stands my son Benjamin, who had followed me. The expression on his face is full of fear.

The ambulance guys come and suddenly we're down the elevator, outside the building, in the ambulance. Someone has given me a sweater. It's the first week of December, a real cold night.

Now we're in the hospital. It's so cold. They take X rays to see what's going on. There is a hemorrhage, a "bleed," in his head. I've worked in a hospital for long enough to know what that means. I know what all these machines are doing, I know what happens to a doctor's face when he can't give good news.

Suddenly I remember that the next day, Jose and Annie go on their class trip to the Big Apple Circus at Lincoln Center. Their father is supposed to be one of the grown-ups who go with them. I call Dani, their teacher, and tell her what's happening, and then I call home to talk to my daughter.

"Don't tell them about their daddy yet, Debbie," I ask. "Let them have this one day." In her tears, she promises she will get them off to the circus, she won't tell them what's going on until I say it's OK.

Five, six hours later, when the doctor shakes his head and says "overwhelming damage," my little bit of hope finally goes away. It's time to let my husband go. After I sign the papers, as the nurses move around the bed unhooking machines, I lean down close to him. "It's all right, Jose," I whisper. "Please don't worry about us, I know what you want me to do. The boy will continue to play his music, and Annie, too, and we'll all be fine. If you have to leave us now, it's OK." The room is quiet, the respirator is off. On the heart monitor, the blips are getting slower.

One of the hospital chaplains comes into the room and looks into my eyes. "You're comfortable with this decision?" she asks quietly.

"Yes," I answer.

"Then don't worry," she tells me. "God is going to help you with this." And I say, "I know," because I did know. And when it's over and my husband's life ends in front of my eyes, I can feel the calm coming in me.

Later, I find out that at almost this exact time, little Jose is really starting to get on his teacher, poor Dani. "Where's my father? He's supposed to be here. Something isn't right." After the circus, on the bus, Jose keeps asking, "What's wrong? I need to be home."

JOSE: Just when we're about to get on the bus, I grab Annie's hand and hold it very, very tight. I know something bad is happening, and I am saying my prayers.

AMERICA: When Dani brings the kids upstairs, we all just look at each other. "Jose, there's a reason your papa didn't come to the circus," Dani says, but then she stops, because his eyes are getting really big. I think, *He knows what's coming.* So I bend down and tell him what happened to his papa, as gentle as I can. He just looks up and then, without saying a word, he goes to his room. In a minute, we hear the violin.

JOSE: I just did a scale, except I did it really sad. It was all I could think of to do. It brought the sadness into me. And I wanted Papa to hear it.

AMERICA: He was in there, all alone, and this soft little violin sound was coming out. Like a voice. Dani said to leave him alone, he would come out when he was ready. And when he did, finally, he was crying, and he and Annie cried together, and then the big kids cried with them.

JOSE: Papa died on December 8, the Feast Day of the Immaculate Conception. And to my heart that was a very hard time for me. I didn't talk or laugh for the whole day. The funeral was on December 11. I kept telling my mom that I had to go right back to school right after we buried my dad. Midori was coming, and I made a commitment with Roberta to play in a concert for Midori. And I was supposed to give her some flowers, to honor her.

AMERICA: I couldn't believe this kid! What was he talking about? Yes, he said, he was leaving the cemetery and going back to school. "Jose, you can't do that," I said. "The family goes back to the house afterward." But there was no changing his mind.

JOSE: When I saw my father's coffin go down into the grave, I said to Mom, "I have to go now." And the flowers they gave me to put on Papa, I only put some of them in, and kept the rest to give to Midori. Everybody was looking at me like, what is that weird kid doing?

All my brothers took me. We went to their cars, Annie came with me, and we left. Then everybody else went to their cars, too, and the funeral limos lined up behind us, and the whole procession took off. Everybody followed us to the school!

AMERICA: There I was on the FDR Drive in the big black limo and I just started to laugh, this kid was so unbelievable. "Look what has happened here," I said to my husband. "Now comes the part I have to do by myself—raising them. And your Jose is leading a parade!"

JOSE: When we pulled up at school, Annie and I jumped out. The funeral cars were lined up behind us! My brothers started to come in with us, but I told them no, it's my responsibility. I went up to Midori and gave her the flowers and a kiss, then I went to play violin with the group, like we planned. Roberta was looking at me. "Jose, this is a hard day for you," she said. "You didn't have to do this." But I did, because I made a commitment. I know my papa didn't mind. Sometimes what you have to do to get through something is do the thing you have to do. It can't

matter how it looks to anybody else. This is
something I've learned.

AMERICA: A few days after the funeral, I found a surprise in
my husband's closet—before he died, he went
Christmas shopping for the kids. There was a
tape cassette player and tapes for Jose, to record
and listen to his own practicing, and to listen to
classical music. There was an electric keyboard
for Annie, because we didn't have the piano then.
Oh, my God, I thought. He finally understood.
He knew.

At Christmas, I felt very alone. The kids were all
around, of course, but there was such sadness in all of
us. I knew that everything had changed, but I didn't
know what the change was, exactly. It was not just that
my husband was gone; it was something to do with Jose
and his music. I knew I was standing at a moment of
choosing—how my life would go, how my kids' lives
would go. And then came a knock at the door, and it
was Allan Miller and Susan Kaplan, from the documentary film team. "We're here," they said. "What do you
need?"

Oh, I was so relieved to see them. "Help me with
this decision," I said. "Do I turn and go backward, or
do I turn and go forward?"

They seemed to understand, maybe from getting to

know us while they were making the documentary, the struggle I was talking about. "What do you *want* to do?" they asked. "Because, America, you can make choices."

I thought about that for a while. More than anything else, I wanted quiet in our lives—some order, some reason. That's when I said, "You know what? From now on, everything will be different."

I have to say the hard truth here—we are Latinos, and the fact is, much of the music the kids play as they learn violin and piano is not from the Spanish culture. It's from the white culture. When they get better or older, they can play whatever, and Jose watches for Latin musicians and composers. But in the beginning, the classics build the foundation for the kids—German, French, Italian composers. So sometimes the trade-off, the balancing, is between my own culture and roots and where I want my kids to go. I worry—will they lose something? Do they have to trade away one part of themselves in order to have this other way of being?

When you make a move to make your life better, sometimes the people around you, the people who should most want good things for you, act like you're trying to cross a mountain that you shouldn't be crossing. With all old friends and family, it's "Who do you think you are? You're getting above yourself, which means you're getting above us—which means you're insulting us. So who do you think you are?" Well, it's simple—we're not the same people we were. I have to go in a direction that will benefit my kids; not just Jose and Anastasia, but also Destiny, my daughter Debbie's child.

My Debbie died of AIDS six months after my husband died. A man she loved and trusted gave it to her, and we didn't know for a long time why she was so sick, or with what. She had Destiny a long time before he made her sick, though. I promised my daughter on her deathbed that I would raise this little girl, keep her healthy and happy, give her the same kind of life that Jose and Annie have. So I adopted her, and she is Jose and Annie's little sister. She is in Roberta's beginner violin class. After school, when Jose and Annie practice, Destiny practices, too.

I learned during this time that you kind of make your family as you go through life. You find other people—like Allan is an uncle, Wally is an uncle, Roberta is an aunt, and Susan is an aunt. This is the family that came to us because of the music. I want my children to know that even though there is so much here in our own culture that is good, there are other people they can learn from.

We have to make some sacrifices to have this— there's only me working now, and we have the lessons, the instruments, the traveling to extra practice sessions. We always celebrated birthdays with a big party and many gifts—now, someone brings a book, some music, and that's plenty. I used to be into clothes; now, I don't care so much about that.

Jose was accepted into Juilliard's Music Advance-

ment Program (MAP) when he was in the third grade—
he got a scholarship. We went there every Saturday for
two years. Now we go to Manhattan School of Music
on Saturdays. During the week, I leave with the kids in
the morning, and I don't come back until seven. At
night, the kids do their homework. Jose practices violin,
Destiny goes *screech, screech*, like Jose did. And Annie
plays her piano. Annie took violin for a little while, but
from the very beginning she liked piano better. When
she plays, it makes such a beautiful sound all through
the apartment; I like to hear it out in the hall when I'm
coming back in from outside. Thursday Jose has orchestra and chamber music. And this is all in addition
to regular schoolwork and homework.

Annie and Jose are in the same class at school, so
sometimes they do their schoolwork together. They
don't fight like some brothers and sisters. There are dis-
agreements, sure. People get mad sometimes—we're
just human beings, after all. But now we try to talk
about this, to find out why, to solve it.

For my older children, when I turned away from the
old way of living, they thought I was rejecting them. No,
that isn't it. "You have to accept the difference between
you and these younger ones," I told them. "They're different because they're coming up in different circumstances. I know another way now—if we do this, we will
all be better for it." So the big kids began to change a
little, too. They support the little ones, they want them
to have good lives.

JOSE: My brothers listen to music they would not listen to before, not just Latin rock or rap. I got all the Guarneri Quartet CDs, so I can hear Arnold, and sometimes my brothers listen with me. They know who the musicians are, the ones I respect. When everyone is together now for dinner or a party, sometimes I'm practicing, or Annie and I play chamber music, and they sit and listen, and it's OK with them. They tease me sometimes still, but they are smiling when they do it.

AMERICA: Roberta was talking about rap one time, about a couple of the parents being so mad that their kids were listening to this stuff. I remember how it was for me, I used to get so mad at my kids— that music felt like it was going to rip right through the wall. And Roberta told the parents, "But it's the sound of their times, it's out there. If you want them to listen to something else, you can't wait for someone else to give it to them— you have to provide it."

JOSE: About nine, nine thirty, it's so quiet here at home. Instead of watching TV, we talk, sometimes we play games. Sometimes we don't want to, but my mom says, "Do your math, do your reading." Like today, it was a snow day and we were home from school, and yeah, we played a little, but we finished our math, too.

AMERICA: Years back, you wouldn't see a piano in this house, or a computer, or all these books. I could not have dreamed that at this time of my life, I would have three little children under my roof, all taking music lessons! And I've never in my life seen a report card like the ones they get now, all A's and B's—Jose tested 99th percentile in math, a 98th percentile in reading. They go outside plenty, too—they throw the football around with their big brothers, and Jose pitches a pretty good baseball.

We went to the movies the other night, and on the way home we walked past Barnes & Noble, and everybody started laughing, "No, no, we can't go in there!" We always spend too much time, too much money. Jose wants one book, he ends up with two. The Greek myths, *Treasure Island.* I get a classical CD, because maybe it's Arnold, maybe it's Itzhak, and we want to hear them, and have that music in the house. Annie joined a book club, and they send her books. They do drama in her class; they write stories and act them out, like plays. She likes writing, and she thinks maybe she wants to be an artist, or a doctor.

JOSE: And I want to be a musician, a professional violinist. Or maybe a composer. I like jazz. Once, for the end-of-the-year concert, I worked on a piece with Roberta, "The Florida Blues." I really like tango music, too. And I took a Suzuki piece and rewrote it and made it jazzy to mix it up with the classical. "Jazz a Latina," I call it.

I'm interested in medicine, because of all the things that were wrong with me, and because of Papa's illness and my sister's. So maybe I could be a doctor. Or a lawyer, so I could help people, mostly from my neighborhood. And I like politics, maybe I could run for the U.S. Senate.

Every single thing they said I couldn't do twelve years ago, I can do now. I compete with myself, my own brain, to make myself the best I can be. Whatever happens, I want to keep meeting people, having friendships with people all over the world. I like E-mail for that.

AMERICA: Because of the violin program, and the success of the documentary, we have been to such amazing places. The kids played in the White House one Christmas, and in Venice, when the documentary was in the Venice Film Festival, Jose played his violin while we were on a gondola! For Fiddlefest in Zurich, the Swiss kids played our national anthem, and now Jose has a pen pal in Switzerland.

You look around at the world that is so old and beautiful—and a little ruined, some places—and you know there is so much more than you ever dreamed. And it's there for your kids, too, if you show them and guide them. Not having any money makes limits, sure. But not choosing—that makes the biggest limit.

Now, even in my own city, I see things that I never in my life knew were here. The museums, and theater, and dance. We go to Central Park and bird-watch, counting the eagles and the owls. And my big kids love to hang with us. We all go out to dinner together. We go to the little kids' recitals. And my big son goes bicycle riding with me. Yes, I have a bicycle, and I go ice skating at the park, too—sometimes with the kids, and sometimes, on a day off when they're in school, I go all by myself. I think, *This is the thing I'm going to do for myself today.* And it's fine. I learned people have to find a way to make a quiet place for themselves, to think, to just be.

The changes made my work life better. You're more free, more relaxed, you feel you've got less problems than a lot of other people. In my job at Mt. Sinai, I help people—I take their blood, I try to make their time at the hospital not so scary. Sometimes they're angry, or the people I work with are angry, but I'm not so much angry these days. Tired? Sure, who isn't? There's never enough time. But when you find a way to have peace in your life and family—to *make* peace—then nothing is that bad.

My first grandson was born yesterday. I told my son, "You have to start making plans for him right now. It's not too soon." We have a dream about our kids—we dream that it's in our power to do everything we can to see them flower. And then you find it's a hard world, it's not a world that makes it easy for these kids. You have to give them ways.

Music—playing music—changes the way people look at this world. Everybody participates and everybody has a goal, someplace the music is supposed to be go-ing. You follow it, and you go there—that's your job. The thing you learn in music is that it takes more than one kind of note. At a certain age, you know, after enough things happen in your life, a person learns some things. For me, it's not about who's the most powerful person in the room anymore. It's about what we're all going to do together, where we're going, and how we're going to get there.

ACKNOWLEDGMENTS

It's impossible to "write a life" without paying tribute to the people who have helped me live it. These words won't do justice or repay kindnesses, but they come with great love and gratitude to the following people:

- My family, the Guasparis and Vitalis: What I know about love, I learned from you.
- Dr. Homer Garretson and Dr. Louis Richardson, my esteemed teachers at Fredonia.
- Bennington Chamber Music Conference—my first chamber music experience and some of the most fun I've ever had.
- Everyone at Musicorda, especially Jackie Melnick for her inspiration and her example.
- Deborah Meier, mentor and visionary, who encouraged me to go for it.
- Joyce Robins, for fine-tuning me and helping me shape my teaching.
- Ed Miller, whose brilliant ideas opened the door for Opus 118 and whose national anthem arrangement brings them to their feet.
- All the directors and board of Opus 118, founding

and present, who give so much time, for so little, on behalf of so many.

- School District 4, for never, ever closing the door on the violin program.
- The staff and administration of Central Park East and River East schools, who tolerate my constant disruptions of their classrooms and allow the violin program to continue.
- Barry Solowey, whose annual "C.P.E. Opera Co." production is truly an example of music education at its best.
- The InterSchool Orchestra, for giving so many students the precious opportunity to play in quality ensembles, regardless of their ability to pay.
- Steve McGhee, ER doctor for musical instruments— for longtime friendship to my family, unfailing support of my program, and endless violin repairs.
- Morry Alter, who broke the story. Thank you for your genuine respect for our community.
- All the professional musicians who have ever participated in Fiddlefest concerts, thank you for your generous gift of time.
- Madonna, for being a real girlfriend.
- Walter Scheuer, for your blessed ability to see every challenge as a wonderful adventure. Wally, this could never have happened without you. "Who would ever think . . . ?"
- Susan Kaplan, a loving, warm, and generous spirit, who gave me the courage to tell the story and solved so many problems along the way.

- Allan Miller, for your vision and creativity in crafting *Small Wonders*, aka, *Fiddlefest*.
- Dorothea and Arnold, early champions, tireless supporters, cherished friends.
- Itzhak and Isaac, eloquent artists and role models. We are all honored by your friendship and support.
- Harvey, Wes, Marianne, and Amy, and everyone involved with making the film. Thank for building an unbelievable platform for all of us to stand on and advocate for kids.
- Meryl Streep, for bringing your passion and your credibility to the crusade for music and arts education for all children. In the movie about your life, can I play you?
- The parents of my students, who have supported me on behalf of their children and also as fearless advocates for the program.
- Diana Wan, our special accompanist, whose musicality enriches all our rehearsals and performances.
- Dani Toomer, Sophia's teacher and mentor, whose unselfish dedication to her students and their families is a blessing.
- Amelia Gold, Lynelle Smith, and Elizabeth Handman, for their excellent teaching. The Three Graces: A. is hysterically funny, L. is thoughtful and wise, and E. is just plain wonderful.
- Rainie Smith, special friend. Our shared joy in teaching music to kids is so worth the fight.
- Ellen Weiss, my dearest friend and NYC sister. Thank you for your gifts of listening, unconditional

love, and the frank opinion that therapy probably wouldn't be a bad idea.

- Sandra Guaspari Rosenthal, dear cousin. For always including me and my kids, and for the magical dress from Barneys.
- Frank English, my mother's beloved companion, for giving my children a wonderful grandfather and for making my mother so happy.
- My brothers Al and Doug—for the encouragement and strength that I get from their pride in me.
- My sister Lois, the most giving person I know.
- My students, for always making me so proud.
- Pamela Gray, you listened with your heart and your screenplay captured the true spirit of our story.
- Larkin Warren, my "holy" ghost writer, who empathized, respected, cared, and protected my story and my family.
- and Mom, thanks for making me get out of bed.

- The documentary film *Small Wonders*, aka, *Fiddle-fest*, which I refer to throughout this book will always hold a special place in the music of my heart. *Small Wonders* is available on Buena Vista Home Entertainment at your local video stores. For nontheatrical distribution call SWANK at 1-800-876-5577.

- For information and inspiration on alternative public schools, I highly recommend *The Power of Their Ideas: Lessons for America from a Small School in Harlem,* by Deborah Meier (Boston: Beacon Press, 1995).

- For current information concerning the status of music education in the schools; for statistics and ongoing scientific research; and for advocacy organizations at local, statewide, and national levels: The National Association for Music Education (MENC), located at 1806 Robert Fulton Drive, Reston, VA 20191; phone 703/860-4000.

On MENC's website homepage (*www.menc.org/index2.html*) you will find a great deal of useful information, as well as the "Lists and Links" button, which

steers you to the list of 52 MENC state offices, the
National School Boards Associations, and VH1's Save
the Music Campaign (which can also be accessed at
www.vh1.com/insidevh1/savethemus/html)

- The Petra Foundation
  P.O. Box 11579
  Washington, D.C. 20008
  202/364-8964

- Opus 118 Music Center
  112 E. 106th Street, Second Floor
  P.O. Box 986
  New York, NY 10029
  212/831-4455
  fax: 212/831-5155
  E-mail: *opus118ny@aol.com*
  website: *opus118.org*

Guaspari-Tzavaras,
Roberta.

Music of the heart.

DATE			